THE WASHINGTON MONUMENT

A PRACTICAL READER
FOR ADULTS

BOOK TWO

BY

JOSEPHINE DWIGHT MASON
Director of Evening Schools and Immigrant Education
Springfield, Massachusetts

AND

GERTRUDE E. O'BRIEN
Teacher, Elementary Schools and Illiterate Adults
Springfield, Massachusetts

ILLUSTRATED BY MARGO SYLVESTER

D. C. HEATH AND COMPANY
BOSTON   NEW YORK   CHICAGO
ATLANTA   SAN FRANCISCO   DALLAS
LONDON

COPYRIGHT, 1931,
BY
JOSEPHINE DWIGHT MASON AND GERTRUDE E. O'BRIEN

No part of the material covered by this
copyright may be reproduced in any form
without written permission of the publisher.

3 K 6

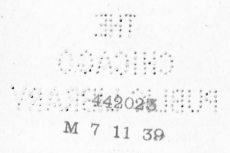
PRINTED IN THE UNITED STATES OF AMERICA

PREFACE

Book Two of *A Practical Reader for Adults* has been written for intermediate classes of illiterate adults, for men and women who have had no education in their own language but who have acquired a simple reading vocabulary, such as is contained in Book One of this series. Because they have been in this country for some time, the majority of these men and women are able to speak and to understand a limited amount of English. Their special need is reading and writing.

The materials and methods of this book, however, are such as to recommend it for use also with pupils of age-level 12–16 who are seriously retarded in reading.

Teachers will find in the accompanying *Teacher's Edition* of Book II detailed suggestions for handling this book in the classroom.

The authors wish to acknowledge their indebtedness to Dr. William S. Gray, Dean of the School of Education, University of Chicago, and to Dr. Zenos E. Scott, Superintendent of Schools, Springfield, Massachusetts, for helpful criticism and constructive suggestions in the development of these three readers.

JOSEPHINE DWIGHT MASON
GERTRUDE E. O'BRIEN

CONTENTS

CONTENTS

A PRACTICAL READER FOR ADULTS

IDENTIFICATION

1. What is your name?
2. What is your address?
3. How old are you?
4. Where were you born?
5. When were you born?
6. How long have you been in the United States?
7. Where do you work?
8. Are you married?
9. How many children have you?
10. When did you come to America?
11. On what boat did you come to America?
12. When did you take out your First Papers?
13. How long have you lived in this state?
14. In case of accident who should be notified?

LESSON 1

SAVING MONEY

Tony wants to go to New York. He wants his brother Sam to go with him, but they will have to save some money before they can go. They are going to put some money in the bank every week. Do you put money in the bank? Their father has money in the bank. He puts some in the first of every month. This is a good way to save. We do not know when we may want the money. Sam bought a new radio with his money, and Tony bought a new house with his money; so they have not saved anything for many months. Tony and

Sam know they can save some money before they will want to take the trip to New York.

Their father and mother are in the new house, and they like the radio. There are so many rooms in their house, they have decided to rent one of them. A friend of Tony's will rent the room. He will like the radio, too.

John, Sam's friend, was in New York week before last, and he told Sam about the good time he had. He told him about all the things he saw, the bright signs, the stores, the movies, and the many many people. He told him, too, about all the things he bought for his family. Sam must take that trip some day. It will be his first trip to New York.

1. They will go to New York next week.
    Yes   No

2. Sam's father has money in the bank.
    Yes   No

3. This is a good way to save. Yes   No

4. Sam bought a new house. Yes   No

5. Tony bought a new radio. Yes   No

6. They decided to rent a room. Yes   No

7. Tony's friend will rent the room. Yes   No

8. John had a good time in New York.
   Yes   No
9. John told about the things he saw.
   Yes   No
10. He told about the things he bought.
    Yes   No
11. It will be Sam's last trip to New York.
    Yes   No

LESSON 2

SAVINGS DEPARTMENT

Tony has decided to open a savings account in the bank. He wants to put his money where it will be safe. Day before yesterday Sam went down to the bank with Tony. Before you can open a savings account, you must make out a card. On this card you must write your name and address. Tony made out his card; he wrote his name and address and gave it to the clerk at the window where it said SAVINGS DEPARTMENT.

The clerk at the window read the card. He wrote Tony's name on a Savings Department bank

book. Tony gave the clerk $5.00. The clerk wrote in the bank book the money that Tony gave him. He gave Tony the bank book. Tony must take this book when he wants to put any money in his savings account.

It is good that so many people save money in this way. Before Tony decided to open a savings account, he had his money in his house. This was not a good thing to do. One day when he came home, he did not find his money. One must work for his money, and one wants to put it where it will be safe. Your money is safe in a good bank.

Tony is glad he put some of his money in a house for his father and mother. Soon he can go to New York.

1. You give the clerk your name and address.
   Yes   No
2. It is good to put your money in your house.
   Yes   No
3. It is good to save money.   Yes   No
4. You must make out a bank book.   Yes   No
5. Tony made $5.00.   Yes   No
6. Tony had his money in his house.   Yes   No
7. One day he found his money.   Yes   No
8. One works for his money.   Yes   No
9. Your money is safe in a good bank.
   Yes   No
10. Soon he can go to New York.   Yes   No
11. At the window it said SAVINGS DEPART-
    MENT.   Yes   No

LESSON 3

THE FIRE

Did you read in the paper the account of the fire next to the bank? The fire was in the store on Main Street. It was in the radio department. The fire department was there before many people found out where the fire was. Tony did

not know about the fire until he read about it
in the paper. He was glad everything was safe in
the bank. Banks are made so that the money
and the other things in the bank will be safe.

Tony saw his foreman in the bank today. He
told Tony he was glad he had put his money in the
bank. His foreman will put some in next week.
He will go down to the bank to the Savings Department and will make out a card. He will give
the card to the clerk. The clerk will write his name
on a bank book. The foreman will take his bank
book to the factory. He wants the men to know
that he puts money in the bank. Many of his
friends put money in the bank every week. They
buy many things for their children with the money

they save in the bank. Some people take trips with the money they save in their savings account.

Tony is glad he can take the trip to New York. He told the men in his factory that they must not leave their money in their houses. It is not safe. He told them that he had his money in his house and that one day when he came home, it was not there. He did not find his money.

1. The fire was next to the _____.
2. Everything was _____ in the bank.
3. Tony saw his _____ go into the bank.
4. He will make out a _____.
5. He will put some money in _____ week.
6. His friends buy many _____ for their children.
7. Some people take _____ with their savings.
8. They save in their savings _____.
9. Tony can go to _____ _____.
10. They must not leave their _____ in their houses.
11. Tony did not find his _____.

LESSON 4

Sam Opens a Savings Account

The other night when Sam went down to the bank, a woman was on the car and she stopped at the bank, too. She is the woman who rented a room in the house of a friend of Sam's. The woman went to the window where it said SAVINGS DEPARTMENT. She gave the clerk some money to put in her savings account. The clerk took her money and her bank book and wrote in it the amount she was putting in that day. The woman's name was on the bank book.

Sam has decided to open a savings account in the bank, too. Last Monday night he went down to the bank. The bank is open Monday nights for those who cannot go there in the daytime. Sam made out a card. He wrote his name and address on it. He gave it to the clerk who was at the window where there was a sign SAVINGS DEPARTMENT. The clerk took Sam's money and his card. He put Sam's name on the bank book and wrote in it the amount of money that Sam gave him. He gave Sam the bank book, and Sam took it home with him. Sam knows his money is safe. The last time Sam was in the bank, he saw that no one was smoking. He knows that no one may smoke in the bank. He did not smoke until he was at home.

Sam is glad the bank is open one night a week for those who cannot go at any other time. On his way home the other night he stopped at the school. His friends there were glad to know that he had put money in the bank. He took some of the cards from the bank to the school and gave them to the men and women in the school. They will make them out. They can all read the cards.

1. The clerk wrote in the bank book the _____ of money.
2. He saw the sign SAVINGS _____.
3. The bank is _____ one night a week.
4. Sam made out a _____.
5. The clerk took Sam's _____.
6. The woman's _____ was on the bank book.
7. On his way home Sam stopped at _____.
8. He gave the _____ to the men and women.

9. They will _____ them out.
10. Sam _____ a savings account.
11. Sam _____ his money is safe.
12. The bank is open at _____ for those who cannot go in the daytime.
13. No one was smoking in the _____.

LESSON 5

RECEIVING

Last night Tony went to the bank to put in some money. The amount he took was $10.00. He had saved that in the last three weeks. He is not going to put this money in his savings account, for he may have to take it out again next week. He is going to put this in his checking account.

He has now two accounts in this bank, a savings account and a checking account. Tonight when he went to the bank, he made out a deposit slip. He wrote on it his name and the amount he was going to deposit. He took the deposit slip, the $10.00, and his bank book, and went to the window where it said RECEIVING.

The teller, who was at the window, took Tony's money, the deposit slip, and his bank book. The teller wrote in his book the amount Tony was depositing, $10.00. Tony took his bank book and went home. When he looks in his bank book, he knows the amount he has deposited.

Did you see the man who came into the bank? That was the man who works next to Tony. He cannot deposit any money now. He has not been well. He will put some money in next week. One of Tony's friends is not well; so, when Tony went to the bank last night, he deposited his friend's money.

1. Tony has saved $10.00 in the last ____ weeks.
2. He took the deposit ____ to the window where it said RECEIVING.
3. Tony has a ____ account and a ____ account.
4. The teller took Tony's ____.
5. Tony may have to take it out ____ week.
6. That was the man who works ____ to Tony.
7. He cannot deposit any money ____.
8. He will put in some ____ next week.
9. Tony deposited his friend's ____.
10. The teller was at the ____.
11. Tony made out a deposit ____.
12. The amount he deposited was ____.

LESSON 6

> CLOSED — NEXT WINDOW

Tony went down to the bank this morning to deposit some money in his checking account. He made out his deposit slip and went to the window where it said RECEIVING. There was a sign on that window that said CLOSED — NEXT WINDOW. Tony went to the next window and de-

posited his money. The teller was receiving the money at that window. Every week Tony has deposited some money in his checking account, and now he has many dollars in it. He has some money in his savings account, too.

Soon Tony and Sam will have saved as many dollars as they must have to go to New York. The factory will be closed for three days soon, and they can go to New York at that time. Their friend John will know the amount of money they must save to go to New York. He was in New York again last month.

As Sam went to work this morning, he saw a friend he knows in school. He is the one who takes him to school in his car. His friend has a closed

car with two doors.   It takes many dollars to buy
a car. He saved the money for this car in his savings account. Next week Sam and his friend will
take a trip in the car.

1. Tony went down to the bank yesterday.
   Yes   No
2. He went to the window where it said SAVINGS
   DEPARTMENT. Yes   No
3. The sign on that window said CLOSED —
   NEXT WINDOW. Yes   No
4. Tony deposited his money at the next window.
   Yes   No
5. Tony has deposited some money in his savings
   account. Yes   No
6. He has money in his savings account.
   Yes   No
7. The factory will be closed for two days.
   Yes   No
8. John will know the amount of money they must
   save. Yes   No
9. Tomorrow Sam and his friend will take a trip.
   Yes   No

LESSON 7

SAM'S BROTHER IS SICK

Sam's brother has been very sick for two months. He has been at home all that time. He has not worked and Sam wants to help him. Sam knows that money will help him very much, and so to-morrow morning he is going down to the bank and will take out some money that he has been depositing. This time he will take the money from his checking account. He will write a check for the amount he will take out, and he will take the money to his brother. The money in his savings account, he will not take out, as he will want that for the trip that he is going to take soon to New York.

Sam is very glad that he has put some money in the bank every week and that he has saved so many dollars, for now he can take some out and help his brother. No one likes to be sick, and no one likes to be out of work. Sam's brother will go to work again next week. He works in a very large factory and goes every morning on the street car. He likes his work very much.

Sam can walk to school when he does not go with his friend in his closed car. It takes him some time to walk, but he likes to walk very much. He can save money, too, as he does not have to go on the street car.

Sam's sister closed her house last week and came to be with their brother when he was sick. She had bought a large house. She liked the house very much, but there was much work in so large a house, and so she decided to close it.

1. Sam's brother has been sick. Yes   No
2. He will take the money from his checking account. Yes   No
3. He will write a check for the amount he will take out. Yes   No
4. He will take the money to his sister.
   Yes   No
5. He wants the money in his savings account for his trip to New York. Yes   No
6. Sam is glad he has saved so few dollars.
   Yes   No
7. Every one likes to be sick. Yes   No

8. Sam's brother will go to work again on Friday.
   Yes   No
9. He goes every morning in a closed car.
   Yes   No

LESSON 8

REVIEW

1. Tony and Sam ____ ____ to save some money.
2. They are going to deposit it in the ____.
3. Day before yesterday Sam ____ down town.
4. Your ____ is safe in a good bank.
5. Did you read the account of the fire in the ____?
6. You must take your bank book ____ you.
7. Tony put his money in the ____ Department.
8. The bank is open at night for those who cannot go in the ____.
9. Tony deposited some money at the ____ where it said RECEIVING.
10. He gave the teller his deposit ____ and his money.
11. He has two ____ in the bank now.
12. Sam's friend has a closed car with ____ doors.

13. He takes him to _____.
14. Tony _____ $10.00.
15. He has many _____ in his checking account.
16. Sam's brother has been sick for two _____.
17. The woman went to the window where it said _____ _____.
18. Sam wrote his name and address on the _____.
19. At first Tony had his money in his _____.
20. One day when he came _____, his money was not there.
21. One must work for his money, and he wants to _____ it.

LESSON 9

Review

1. Tony wants to go to New York. True False
2. Tony and Sam will put some money in the school. True False
3. Their father has money in the bank.
   True False
4. His money is in a good bank. True False
5. He did not write his name and address.
   True False

6. Tony decided to open a savings account.
   True   False

7. Tony had his money in the house.
   True   False

8. He did not find his money. True   False

9. One must work to have money.
   True   False

10. Tony's foreman was glad he had money in the bank. True   False

11. Some people take trips with the money they have saved. True   False

12. Banks are not safe. True   False

13. The bank is open two nights a week.
    True   False

14. It said NO ADMITTANCE on the window.
    True   False

15. Sam made out a card. True   False

16. The people can all read the card.
    True   False

17. The teller was not at the window.
    True   False

18. Tony has three accounts in the bank now.
    True   False

19. He deposited the money where it said RE-CEIVING. True   False

20. Tony has saved $10.00 in three weeks.
    True   False
21. The sign said CLOSED — NEXT WIN-
    DOW. True   False
22. He has no dollars in his checking account.
    True   False
23. Tony went to the bank this morning.
    True   False
24. Sam's brother was sick.   True   False
25. His sister's house is not very large.
    True   False
26. Sam will want the money for his trip to New
    York. True   False
27. It takes many dollars to buy a closed car.
    True   False
28. Sam and his friend will take a trip in his car.
    True   False

LESSON 10

PAYING

Last Monday night Sam went down to the bank
and took out some money for his brother. His account is not very large, but he made out a check for

$25.00 and took it to the window where it said PAYING. Sam gave the teller his check. The teller looked at the check, and he looked at Sam. The teller knows Sam, for he has been in the bank many times. The teller gave Sam the $25.00 in bills.

He gave Sam one $5.00 bill and two $10.00 bills. Sam took the money to his brother, who has been sick. His brother was very glad to have the money. Now he can pay some of his bills. He has been sick so much, he has not worked for two months. He will be very glad to pay his bills.

Sam pays his bills by check. It is a good way to do. He is glad he learned how to make out a check at school. Many of the men and women at school

have checking accounts, and they are glad to know
how to make out a check.

On Monday night the bank is not open until 7.
It is closed at 9 P.M. Tony's friend told him that
his bank is open on Friday nights. He told Tony,
too, that he is paying $25.00 every month on his
house. He has a large house, but he likes it very
much.

1.   When did Sam go to the bank?
2.   What did he do at the bank?
3.   What did he make out?
4.   Where did he take it?
5.   What did Sam give the teller?
6.   What did the teller give Sam?
7.   What were the bills?
8.   Why was Sam's brother glad to have the
      money?
9.   What will he do with the money?
10. How will Sam pay his bills?
11. Where did he learn to make out a check?
12. Many men and women have what?
13. When is the bank open at night?
14. When is the bank of Tony's friend open?
15. What is he paying on his house?

LESSON 11

Taking Out Money

Tony and Sam have now saved enough money;
so they can go to New York. Thursday morning
Tony went down to the bank and took some money
out of his savings account. He went to the window
where it said PAYING. He told the clerk he
wanted to take out $100.00. He gave the clerk
his savings-account bank book.

The clerk wrote the amount Tony wanted on a
slip of paper and Tony signed his name to the
paper. He told the clerk that he wanted the
money in ten-dollar bills. The clerk gave him
the amount, paying him in ten-dollar bills. The
clerk wrote in Tony's bank book that he had paid
him $100.00. Tony was very careful of those ten
ten-dollar bills.

Tony and Sam want enough money for their trip.
They will have to have enough for their tickets and
enough for all the things they will want to buy.
If they have not enough money, Tony will take his

check book with him and he can make out a check.

If Sam has time tomorrow, he is going to find out about the trains. As this will be Sam's first trip to New York, he wants to see as many things as he has time and money for. Tony will buy their tickets tomorrow if he has time. If not, he will buy them when he goes to the train.

Sam's brother is well enough now to go to work. Sam is glad he helped his brother pay his bills when he was sick. Their father is glad Sam and Tony can go to New York.

1. How much money have Tony and Sam saved?
2. When did Tony go to the bank?
3. How did he take out his money?
4. What did the clerk do?
5. How did Tony want the money?
6. How many bills did the clerk give Tony?
7. What will they do if they haven't enough money?
8. What will Sam do tomorrow?
9. How is Sam's brother?
10. Why is Sam glad?
11. What did the clerk write on the slip of paper?
12. How many times has Sam been to New York?

LESSON 12

A LETTER FROM SAM

My dear Brother:

Tony and I arrived here in New York City last night.   We had a very good time on the train. We went through some very large cities.   As we went through one of the cities, we saw, from the car window, many stores and houses.   In one city that we went through, we saw five factories.   Many men and women work in those factories.   They were going home when we saw them.   They looked as if they were glad they had work.

Before the train pulled out of the depot, we bought a New York paper.   We read it on the train and found out about all the things that were going on in the city.   We read, too, the ads of the sales in the city stores.   We read what are to be at the theaters and the movies.   If we have enough time, we shall go into some of the stores tomorrow morning.

The first thing we did last night was to go out

and walk up and down the streets. We started up one street and then went down the next. We saw many bright signs. Some of the streets were as bright as day. We saw ten stores open, but the large stores were all closed. Tony said if he had money enough, he would like to be in New York all the time. The people in this city look as if they had very much money. There must be many very large banks in New York. We saw five banks as we walked down the street.

Tomorrow morning we shall go into some of the large stores. We went up town last night, and tomorrow we shall go down town. There are many things to see here, and Tony and I want to see every one. Some day you must come here with us. We shall want to come again soon.

We shall telegraph you when we shall arrive home, and you must tell father and mother.

Yours truly,

Sam

LESSON 13

A LETTER FROM TONY

My dear Friend:

Sam and I have been in New York for five days.
We came to the city on Friday. We have seen
many, many things. You know this is my first trip
to New York, and so I wanted to go everywhere
and to see everything, as long as I had enough
money. We have been up and down the city
at night, and we have been up and down it in
the daytime. We have walked, and we have been
on the cars. We have walked through many
streets.

Day before yesterday we thought we would go
up in one of the large buildings. We went way up
until we came to the top of the building. From the
top we looked way down the city. We thought we
saw a train. Then we looked way up the city.
The people in the streets looked very small to us.
The cars looked very small to us, too. The buildings here are very large, and you look way up to

the top of them. We do not have so large build-ings at home. The buildings at home are small.

Some of the streets here are very long. On one street we saw a church, and we went into it. The church had many lovely windows in it. We were a long time in that church. We went up and looked at every window. We thought they were lovely.

One night we went to the theater, and we saw a good picture. The signs at the entrance were very bright. A long sign at the top of the door told us what the picture was about. Sam and I saw many EXIT signs in the theater. We knew that we must go out of one of those doors. We saw many men and women at the movies. Many were on the street wanting to go in. We thought we should like to see that picture again.

Sam and I are going home on Wednesday. We have had a very good time. As soon as we can save enough money, we shall want to come to New York again. The next time we come, we want to be here a long time.

Save your money so you can come with us.

Yours truly,
Tony

LESSON 14

A Conversation

" Good morning, John."

" Good morning, Sam. Isn't this a lovely morning? A friend told me that you and Tony had been
to New York. Did you have a good time? When
did you come back? "

" Oh, yes. Tony and I went to New York, and
we had the best time. We came back here last
week."

" Had you been in New York before? "

" No, this was my first trip. I have thought
about going to New York for a long time, but this is

the first time that I have saved enough money to take the trip."

" How did you save the money? "

" I saved the money in the bank. We are paid on Saturdays. Every Monday night I went down to the bank and put some money in my savings account. By putting some in every week, it wasn't long before I had enough for this trip."

" I put money in a checking account. How would I put some in a savings account? "

" Any one of the savings banks will be glad to have you open an account with them. This is what you do. When you have some money to deposit, you go down to the bank and go to the window where it says SAVINGS DEPARTMENT. The clerk there will give you a card to make out. You make out this card and sign your name and address. Then you give it and your money to the clerk at the window. The clerk will write your name on a savings-department bank book, and he will write in the book the amount you give him. The clerk will give you back the bank book. You must take the bank book with you every time you deposit any money in your savings account. It is the best way I know of to save money."

" I am so glad, Sam, to have this information about putting money in the savings bank. But you haven't told me about your trip to New York. What did you and Tony do there? "

" Tony and I did every thing we had enough money for. New York is a very large city, and we did not have time or money enough to see all we wanted to. We arrived at night, and the first thing we did was to go out and see the city by night. We walked up and down the streets and looked at all the bright signs. We thought that many of the signs looked like pictures. There was one sign that we liked and every night we would look for it."

" Did you go into any of the stores? "

" Oh yes, we went into many of the stores. We bought some things for the children. Tony bought a new suit and I bought a new hat. We liked the things we bought. The stores were very large, and there were many people in them."

" Did you go into any of the office buildings? "

" Yes, we went up in one of the office buildings. We went way up until we came to the top. From the top we looked up and down the city. Every one and every thing looked very small to us from way up there. It was a long way to the top of the building, and it took us a long time to come down again."

" Did you go into any of the churches? "

" Yes, we went into three churches. The one we liked the best had very lovely windows in it. It was a large church, but the building next to it was a small one. You do not see very many small buildings in New York, and the large ones are very, very large."

" I must open a savings account and save my money, so I can go to New York. It will be my first trip to New York, too."

" Yes, you must go to New York, for it was the best trip I have had. Now that we are back, I want to go to New York again to see the things we didn't have time or money for on this trip."

" Good-by, Sam. I'm glad I saw you this morning. I'm so glad to know all about your trip. If you go again, I want to know about it. If I can save enough money, I want to go with you. I am going down to the bank on Monday night and open a savings account."

" Good-by, John. We shall be glad to have you go with us. Do start a savings account next Monday night."

LESSON 15

VACATION CLUB

Last Monday night when Sam went to the bank to put some money in his savings account, he saw a large sign VACATION CLUB. He had come back from his vacation; so he thought that he was not interested in a Vacation Club.

When he went to the window to deposit his money, the clerk said to him: " Good evening, I hear you and your brother are back from a trip to New York. Can't I interest you in putting a few dollars each week into our Vacation Club? "

" No," said Sam. " I'm not interested in that club. You see I had deposited some money in my savings account, and so, when I went to New York, I took that money out. Now I have come back from my vacation, and I have no money left after the trip. That is why I am not interested in the club."

" That is why I thought you would be interested in the Vacation Club," said the clerk. " You put in a few dollars each week and then when you want to take a trip, the money will all be saved, and you will not have to take the money out of your savings account. You can take the vacation you want, for you will know how much money you have in your Vacation Club account."

" You make me want to put money in a Vacation Club after all," said Sam. " How much do I have to put in each week? I want to go to Washington some time. If I join a Vacation Club, shall I have money enough to go there? It may be the best way to save money for the trip."

" You can put in a dollar each week for fifty weeks," said the clerk, " and you will have fifty dollars. If you want a larger amount for your vacation, you must deposit a larger amount of

money each week. It is the best way to save
money for your vacation."

"I am glad you told me about the club," said
Sam. "I am going to join the club tonight. Here
is $5.00. I shall go home and tell Tony I have
joined a Vacation Club."

1. What sign did Sam see?
2. Where had Sam been?
3. What did the clerk say to Sam?
4. Why wasn't Sam interested in joining a club?
5. Where had he saved his money?
6. What did the clerk tell him?
7. When must he put the money in the bank?
8. Why will the money be saved?
9. What can you plan?
10. How will you know how much money you have
    for your vacation?
11. What did Sam want to do?
12. Where did Sam want to go?
13. Is it a good way to save for a vacation?
14. What did Sam say about joining the club?
15. How much money did he give the clerk?

LESSON 16

CHRISTMAS CLUB

Sam is so glad that he joined the Vacation Club. Now if he wants to go to Washington, he will have the money. He wants very much to have Tony join the Vacation Club, too, and then he can go to Washington with him.

When Sam went to the factory yesterday, he told a few of his friends that he had joined the Vacation Club. They were all very much interested. Sam told them just why he had joined the club.

One of the men told Sam that he had joined the Christmas Club. Sam didn't know anything about the Christmas Club, but the other night, when he went down to the bank, he saw the sign CHRIST-MAS CLUB at one of the windows.

The man who has joined the Christmas Club told Sam that he puts in a dollar a week for fifty weeks. Just before Christmas, the bank sends him a check for fifty dollars. He has that money to spend for Christmas. That is why he is glad to put money in the Christmas Club. He can buy something for Christmas for each one of his family. He likes to spend his money for Christmas.

The banks help people to save money. They can put their money in many accounts. Sam did not know before that there were so many ways to save money. Sam will be interested in joining a Christmas Club. When he goes to the bank the next time, he will ask the clerk to give him information about the Christmas Club. He will put in a few dollars each week, and then, just before Christmas, he will receive a check from the bank.

1. What club has Sam joined?
2. What does he want Tony to do?

3. What did one of the men tell Sam?
4. How much does he put in each week?
5. For whom does he spend his money?
6. What do the banks do?
7. What didn't Sam know?
8. In what is Sam interested now?
9. What will he do?
10. What will he receive?

LESSON 17

Review

1. Going through one city, they saw _____.
   many stores   five factories
   many children

2. They read the paper to see what was going on in the _____.
   schools   city   depot

3. Last night they saw on the streets _____.
   bright lights   high buildings
   many people

4. Tomorrow they will go into some _____.
   stores   buildings   churches

5. Sam has been to New York _____.
   once   twice   never

6. In the buildings we went to the _____.
   first floor   top   entrance

7. From the top the people looked _____.
   very large   very small   lovely

8. They went into the stores _____.
   yesterday   today   day before yesterday

9. The church had _____.
   lovely windows   a large door
long windows

10. Sam was not interested in a Vacation Club because _____.
    he did not need any money
    he had money in the Vacation Club
    he had come back from his vacation

11. Sam wants to go for a vacation to _____.
    New York   Chicago   Washington

12. You put in a dollar a week and you will have _____.
    ten dollars   fifty dollars
one hundred dollars

13. In the Vacation Club you save for a _____.
    house   church   vacation

14. Sam told his friends he had joined the _____.
    Vacation Club   Christmas Club
          School Club

15. Sam saw the sign _____.
    VACATION CLUB   CHRISTMAS CLUB
          SCHOOL CLUB

16. The bank _____.
    helps people to save their money
    keeps the money to spend
    gives you information about trains

17. Just before Christmas you will _____.
    take a trip   go to school   receive a check

18. Tony and Sam _____.
    went to see some factories
    had a good time on their trip
    did not have enough money

19. They saw in New York some large _____.
          streets   banks   depots

LESSON 18

Review

1. Tony wants to go to New York.
   True   False

2. He is going to put money in the bank every month. True   False

3. John did not have a good time in New York.
   True   False

4. Your money is safe in a good bank.
   True   False

5. One does not have to have work to have money.
   True   False

6. The bank is open every night. True   False

7. You must take your savings-account bank book. True   False

8. I draw checks on my savings account.
   True   False

9. CLOSED — NEXT WINDOW means I must go to another window. True   False

10. We went to New York on the bus.
    True   False

11. They saved enough money to go to Boston.
    True   False
12. They bought a Chicago paper.
    True   False
13. They did not go out on the first night.
    True   False
14. They did not have a good time in New York.
    True   False
15. Sam put money for Christmas in his Vacation
    Club account.   True   False
16. Tony pays his bills by check.   True   False
17. The teller is the man who takes your money.
    True   False
18. They went down in the office building.
    True   False
19. The lights in the morning were very bright.
    True   False
20. They bought some things for the children.
    True   False
21. The bank helps people to save hats.
    True   False
22. Sam gave some money to his sister.
    True   False
23. The bank sends the Christmas money by
    check.   True   False

24. Sam's friend has an open car.   True   False
25. They did everything they had money enough
    for. True   False
26. This was their first trip to New York.
    True   False
27. Sam is glad he joined the Vacation Club.
    True   False

LESSON 19

SIGHT READING

THE WOMAN AND HER HEN

A woman had a very fine hen. This hen laid one large egg every morning. On Saturday the woman would take her seven eggs to market and would sell them for a good price. With the money she would buy herself something nice to wear.

One day as she was going to market, she said to herself: " The people are always glad to buy my eggs, and they will pay me a good price for them. If I had twice as many eggs, I would have twice as much money." She thought of this for many days and tried to think of a way she could get the hen to lay more eggs. At last she decided what she would do.

She said to herself: " Tomorrow I shall give my hen twice as much food and then she will lay twice as many eggs. Then I shall sell them, and I shall have twice as much money." The woman was very much pleased with her plan, and she started right off to market to get more food for the hen.

The next day she began giving more food to the hen. She gave her twice as much as she had ever given her before. Then the woman waited to see what would happen. But each day the hen laid only one egg.

However, the woman kept on giving the hen more and more food, and the hen grew fatter and fatter. But she laid only one egg each day. At last the hen grew so fat she didn't lay any more eggs.

The woman had spent twice as much money for food, but now she had no eggs at all.

1. The woman had a fine ____.
2. One day she was going to ____.
3. The hen laid ____ large egg every morning.
4. The woman would sell them for a ____ price.

5. If I had ____ as many eggs, I would have ____ as much money.
6. I shall give my hen twice as much ____.
7. She waited to see what would ____.
8. The hen grew ____ and ____.
9. She laid only ____ egg.
10. She didn't lay any ____ eggs.

LESSON 20

STAMPS

MONEY ORDERS   LETTERS

Mrs. White wanted to send some money to New York. Her teacher at school told her to go to the post office and send a money order. Her teacher told her to go to the Money Order window and ask the clerk for a blank to fill out. She told her that the clerk would take her money and give her back her money order and a receipt. She told her to put the money order in her letter and the receipt for the money in her bag.

The next morning Mrs. White went down to the

post office. She looked for the window with the sign MONEY ORDERS, and went to that window as her teacher had told her to do. She asked the clerk for a money order blank to fill out. The clerk gave her the blank. She filled out the blank and gave it and the money to the clerk. The clerk made out the money order and gave it and the receipt to Mrs. White.

Mrs. White put the money order in her letter, and the receipt that he gave her, she put in her bag. She had no stamp for her letter; so she went to the window that said STAMPS and bought five of them. She put one on her letter and the others in her bag with the receipt. She mailed the letter at the window where it said LETTERS.

Mrs. White will have the other stamps to put on the next letters she sends to New York. Her friend works in New York, and Mrs. White writes to her every week.

1. Mrs. White wants to send some _____ to New York.

      books   hats   money

2. She went to the _____ _____ for a money order.

      post office   new store   big factory

3. The clerk gave her a _____ to fill out.

      book   blank   card

4. Mrs. White _____ the blank out.

      fill   filled   wrote

5. Mrs. White put the _____ in her bag.

      blank   receipt   card

LESSON 21

REGISTERED LETTERS

Mrs. White has a friend in Boston. Her name is Betty. Mrs. White would like to have her friend Betty come and see her for a few days; so she wants to send her a ticket.

The ticket costs money, and Mrs. White does not want it lost in the mail. She asked her teacher if she should send a money order for the cost of the ticket, or if she should send the ticket. The teacher told her to write a letter to Betty and ask her to come to see her and to put the ticket in the letter, then to take the letter to the window in the post office where it says REGISTERED LETTERS and send it by registered mail. Then it will not be lost.

The next morning Mrs. White wrote the letter. Then she went down to the depot and bought the ticket. She put the ticket in the letter and put a stamp on the letter. Then she went to the post office and found the window with the sign REGIS–

TERED LETTERS on it. She did not have to fill out a blank. The clerk took her letter and registered it. He filled out the blank and gave Mrs. White the receipt. She paid the clerk fifteen cents. She put the receipt in her bag. She knows that her letter will not be lost in the mail.

When Betty receives the ticket, she will write Mrs. White and tell her when she will arrive. Mrs. White will want to be at the depot when she arrives. They will do many things when Betty comes.

1. Mrs. White has a ＿＿ in Boston.
2. She asked her teacher if she should send a ＿＿ ＿＿ for the cost of the ticket.
3. Mrs. White mailed a ＿＿ to her friend.
4. She sent it by ＿＿ ＿＿.
5. She does not want it to get ＿＿.
6. She went to the ＿＿ and bought the ticket.
7. She went to the post office to the window where it said ＿＿ ＿＿.
8. The ticket costs ＿＿ money.
9. She put the receipt in her ＿＿.

LESSON 22

Meeting Betty

Mr. and Mrs. White went to the depot to meet Betty. They did not want her lost. They were a few minutes late, but the train was not on time. It was a few minutes late, too. They waited in the depot.

As they waited, they looked at the many signs. They saw the signs, TICKETS, INFORMATION, and many others. They saw a man writing a telegram. They saw Mr. White's teacher waiting for a train, too.

In a few minutes the late train arrived. Betty

was glad that they had come to meet her. Mr. White took her bag and they all walked to Main Street.

Mr. White had to go to the post office; so Betty and Mrs. White waited out in front. Mr. White went in to send a money order. At first he didn't find the window, as all the departments had been moved. He read the signs and found the money order window. It is now in the back of the post office. The stamps are next to the window where you mail your letters. The window where you register your letters is in the front of the post office. Mr. White was glad that there were signs at all the windows. If he hadn't learned to read the signs, he wouldn't have known where to go for the money order or the stamps. Every one should learn to read the signs.

Mr. White gave the receipt for the money order to Mrs. White, and she put it in her bag, so it would not be lost. They went home in Mr. White's closed car. Tomorrow Mrs. White will take Betty down town to see the stores.

1. The train was on time.   True   False
2. Mr. and Mrs. White were late.   True   False

3. They saw the sign EXIT.   True   False
4. They saw a man writing a telegram.
   True   False
5. Mrs. White had to go to the post office.
   True   False
6. Betty and Mrs. White waited in the back of the
   post office. True   False
7. Mr. White couldn't find the money order window. True   False
8. Mr. White couldn't read the signs.
   True   False
9. They went home on the street car.
   True   False

LESSON 23

A Trip Down Town

This morning Mrs. White and Betty went down
town.   Mrs. White took her friend to see the new
bank, the theaters, the church, and the stores.
They went in the new bank to cash a check. Betty
waited next to one of the front windows.

Mr. and Mrs. White have a checking account
and also a savings account in this bank. They are

careful to save a little money each month. It took a few minutes for Mrs. White to write out her check and take it to the front paying window where she received cash for it.

When they left the bank, they went through the stores. Betty wanted to buy a new hat and also something for each of her children. One of her girls wanted a blue dress. The other girl had lost her bag and wanted a new brown one. Her boy wanted some brown shoes.

They saw many lovely things. Some of the dresses were ten dollars. Betty bought one for her girl. It was a lovely blue. She bought also some brown shoes for her boy. She paid cash for all the things.

It was not late when they were through; so they went to the movies. The pictures were very good, but they were long. Mr. White was at home when they arrived. He was listening to the radio. Betty helped Mrs. White, and in just a few minutes they had supper.

Betty showed Mr. White the things that she had bought. She said that her boy had to have new shoes every month. Mr. White liked the blue dress. He asked Betty how much it had cost.

In the evening they listened to the radio. Betty liked to listen to it. Mr. White had bought the radio just in the last month. Mrs. White and he listened to it every evening.

1. Mrs. White and Betty went in the new ____ to cash a check.
2. Mr. and Mrs. White ____ a little each month.
3. Betty bought some ____ shoes.
4. She bought a ____ dress.
5. She paid ____ for the things.
6. Betty's boy had to have new shoes every ____.
7. In the evening they listen to the ____.
8. Mr. White liked the blue ____.

LESSON 24

PARCEL POST

Last night Betty wrote a letter to her mother in Italy. She also wrote to her girls. She put the brown shoes which she had bought for her son in a box and addressed it to him. She also put the girl's new things in a box, but she did not mail

them. She knew she would take those home with her.

Mr. White took her to the post office in his closed car. She went first to the window that said PARCEL POST. She mailed there the shoes to her son. It cost 15¢ to send the shoes by parcel post. Then Betty went to the window where it said STAMPS and bought two five-cent stamps. It costs five cents to send a letter to Italy. She put one stamp on the letter to her mother, and the other she put in her bag. She would have that one ready to put on the next letter she wrote to her mother.

Betty took her letter to the window where it said LETTERS and mailed it. She knew that it would go on a train to New York and then on to Italy. She knew also that it would be many days before her mother would receive the letter.

Mr. White took Betty to the telegraph office, where she sent a telegram which said that she would arrive home at 2 P.M. the next day. Her son will meet the train. He will be there to help her with her bag and with the box of things for the girls.

1. Betty wrote to her mother in _____.
2. She put the brown _____ in a box.
3. She mailed them at the parcel post _____.
4. It cost her 15¢ to send the _____.
5. It cost her 5¢ to send the _____.
6. She mailed the letter where it said _____.
7. She _____ that it would go on a train.
8. Then it would go on to _____.
9. She sent a _____.
10. She is going home _____.
11. Her _____ will meet her.
12. He will help her with her _____.
13. Mr. White has a _____ car.
14. He took Betty to the _____ _____.

LESSON 25

REVIEW

1. Mrs. White wanted to send a ticket to New York.   True   False

2. She went to the STAMP window to make out her money order.   True   False

3. The clerk gave her a blank to fill out.
   True   False

4. She sent the receipt in the letter.
   True   False

5. She writes to her friend every week.
   True   False

6. Mrs. White has a friend in Boston.
   True   False

7. She will send her a ticket by parcel post.
   True   False

8. She does not want it lost.   True   False

9. She will register her letter in the depot.
   True   False

10. The train was a few minutes late.
   True   False

11. Mr. White had to go to the post office.
    True   False

12. They had not moved any department in the
    post office.   True   False

13. You register your letters at the stamp window.
    True   False

14. Mr. White wanted to send a money order.
    True   False

15. Mrs. White went to the theater to cash a check.
    True   False

16. Betty bought her son some blue shoes.
    True   False

17. They saw a good picture at the movie.
    True   False

18. Mr. White was listening to the radio.
    True   False

19. The girl's dresses cost $25.00.   True   False

20. Mr. White took Betty to the post office to mail
    her box.   True   False

21. Betty wrote to her mother in Italy.
    True   False

22. It costs 2¢ to send a letter to Italy.
    True   False

23. Betty bought her girl a brown dress.
    True   False

24. Her girl will meet the train.　True　　False
25. Her son will help her with her bag.
    True　　False
26. Mr. White bought his radio last year.
    True　　False
27. He never listens to it.　True　　False

LESSON 26

REVIEW

1. Mrs. White's teacher told her to send the _____ by registered mail.

   　　　book　　ticket　　receipt

2. She would have to go to the _____ _____ to do this.

   　savings bank　　post office　　movies

3. The clerk would give her a _____ to fill out.

   　　　card　　book　　blank

4. She would keep the _____.

   　　　blank　　receipt　　card

5. You mail your letters at the window that says _____.

   LETTERS　STAMPS　MONEY ORDERS

6. You buy stamps at the window that says ____.

    LETTERS STAMPS MONEY ORDERS

7. You buy a ticket at the ____.

    post office depot bank

8. She knew the ticket would not be ____.

    bought read lost

9. Mrs. White wants to be at the train when Betty ____.

    leaves arrives goes

10. You would see ____ in the depot.

    STAMPS PARCEL POST TICKETS

11. You would see ____ in the depot.

    INFORMATION SMOKING LETTERS

12. The train was ____.

    going late sick

13. Mrs. White and Betty went to the bank to ____ a check.

    cash buy read

14. Mr. and Mrs. White have ____ accounts in the bank.

    one two three

15. Betty bought some ____ shoes for her son.

    white blue brown

16. She bought a ____ dress for her girl.

    white blue brown

17. One sends a box through the mail by _____ _____.

    money order   cash   parcel post

18. Betty's son will help her with her _____.

    stamps   letters   bag

19. They saw a man writing a _____.

    letter   blank   telegram

20. It costs 5¢ to send a letter to _____.

    New York   Boston   Italy

21. It takes a long time for a letter to go to _____.

    New York   Boston   Italy

22. Mr. and Mrs. White listen to the radio every _____.

    morning   day   evening

LESSON 27

SIGHT READING

THE FISHERMAN AND THE LITTLE FISH

One hot morning in summer a fisherman took his pole and went to a brook not far away to catch some fish. He fished all day but did not get a single bite. " I will try once more before going home," he said. He threw in his line, and it wasn't long before he felt a little pull on it. This made him very happy, and he pulled in his line very carefully, so he wouldn't lose the fish.

Sure enough, there was a fish at the end of the line, but it was a very small fish. The little fish was very much frightened at finding himself out of the water and called out, " Oh, Sir, take pity on me, for I'm such a small fish. Please throw me back in the water again. See what a little thing I am. I shall not make even a mouthful for you now. If you leave me in the water, I shall grow some more, and then I shall be worth catching. You can make a good dinner of me then or you can sell me for a good price."

" Ah, that is true," said the fisherman, " you are very small and you will only make me a mouthful now, but I have you safely here in my basket. If I put you back in the water, I might never catch you again. As small as you are, you are better than nothing and I shall keep you."

The little fish lay down in the basket and that night the fisherman had him for his supper.

1. One morning a fisherman went out to fish.
   True   False

2. He fished one hour. True   False
3. When he felt a pull on his line, it made him feel sad.   True   False
4. He pulled in his line carefully. True   False
5. There was a large fish on the end of the line. True   False
6. The fish asked the fisherman to throw him back. True   False
7. The fisherman said, " You are very large and you will make me a good dinner." True   False
8. He said, " Small as you are, you are better than nothing." True   False
9. He said to the fish, " I shall not keep you." True   False

LESSON 28

OBEY THE TRAFFIC SIGNALS

The other day as Tony was going home from work, he saw a bad accident. A boy was going across the street, and he did not obey the traffic signals. The traffic officer had put up his hand and

signaled the people to stop. Then he signaled the street cars and the automobiles to go.

A boy who had a large parcel in his hand and who was on his way to the post office to mail it, thought he could run across the street before the cars and the automobiles started. The boy started to run, but before the traffic officer could stop him, he was hit by an automobile.

All the cars and the automobiles stopped then, but it was too late, for the boy had been hit. He did not obey the signal of the traffic officer.

It was a bad accident and they took the boy home. He was sick for a week. The days were long for him, and he thought many times about the accident. The next time he goes out, he will obey the traffic signals.

Tony knows the boy's father. He works next to him in the factory; so Tony went to see the boy last night. He found the boy better. He was putting stamps in his stamp book. He likes to save stamps and has a good many in his stamp book.

Tony took a book to him to read. The boy told Tony that he could go to school next week. Tony told the boy that the next time he started to cross the street, it would be better for him to look first at the signals.

1. The accident was a ____ one.
2. He did not ____ the signals.
3. The traffic officer had put up his ____.
4. The boy had a ____ in his hand.
5. The boy ____ to run across the street.
6. The boy was hit by an ____.
7. Obey the traffic ____.
8. Tony knows the boy's ____.
9. The boy was putting ____ in his stamp book.
10. He has a good ____ stamps.
11. He thought many times about the ____.

LESSON 29

Don't Hang Anything Over the Stove

Mrs. Bruno had just washed out some things and hung them over the stove to dry. She went out in front of the house to wait for the things to dry. From her house Mrs. Bruno could see the traffic officer on the next street. She liked to see him put up his hand and then see all the street cars and the automobiles stop. The people would stop, too.

Some of Mrs. Bruno's friends came out and waited in front with her. They had been down town and told her about the things they had bought at the store.

They had not been out in front very long when they heard a great noise. Every one was looking down the street. Mrs. Bruno and her friends looked down the street, too. They saw the fire engines. The fire engines were coming down their street. The traffic officer signaled everyone to stop. The street cars and the automobiles all stopped, and no one crossed the street.

The engines came nearer and nearer, and the noise was very great. Mrs. Bruno and her friends looked to see where the engines were going. Just as they came in front of Mrs. Bruno's house, the engines stopped and the firemen ran into her house.

It was not a large fire, and the firemen put it out in a few minutes, but all the things that hung over the stove were burned.

As the firemen left the house, one of them said to Mrs. Bruno: " Don't hang anything over the stove to dry. If the fire engine house had not been so near, your house would have burned down." What the fireman said was true, and Mrs. Bruno knew that it was true. The next time she washes, she will not hang anything over the stove to dry.

1. Mrs. Bruno had just _____.
2. She hung the things over the _____.
3. She wanted them to _____.
4. Mrs. Bruno could see the traffic _____.
5. Some _____ came to see her.
6. They had been to the _____.
7. They heard a great _____.
8. They looked _____ the street.
9. They saw the fire _____.
10. The traffic officer signaled every one to _____.
11. The engines came _____ and _____.
12. They stopped in front of _____ _____ _____.
13. The _____ ran into her house.
14. It was not a _____ fire.
15. The firemen put it out in a few _____.
16. All the things that hung over the stove were
    _____.
17. " Don't hang anything over the _____."
18. " Your house would have _____ down."
19. What the firemen said was _____.
20. Mrs. Bruno knew that it was _____.
21. The next time she _____, she will not _____ any-
    thing over the stove.

LESSON 30

KNOW HOW TO RING IN A FIRE ALARM

It was the ashman, taking the ashes out of Mrs. Bruno's house, who saw the smoke coming out of Mrs. Bruno's back window. The ashman knew that there was a fire alarm box on the next corner. He ran out to it to ring in the alarm. He knew how to ring it in.

On the box it said:

```
BREAK   THE   GLASS
TURN  THE  HANDLE
OPEN    THE    DOOR
PULL     THE     HOOK
DOWN   ONCE   AND
       LET  GO
```

The ashman did this. He hit the glass, to break it; then he turned the handle; he opened the door; he pulled the hook down once, and then he let go of it.

He knew that he would not hear the alarm ring, but he knew that he must wait to tell the firemen where the fire was.

Soon he heard a great noise. The fire engines were coming down the street. They came to the corner where the fire alarm box was, and the ashman told the firemen that the fire was in Mrs. Bruno's house. Then the ashman went to help the firemen.

Mrs. Bruno was glad the man had seen the smoke in time and that he knew how to ring in the alarm. He had saved her house for her.   It had not burned down.

When any one rings in the fire alarm, he must wait at the box until the firemen arrive or they will not know where the fire is.

1. The smoke came out of the _____ window.
2. He knew how to ring in the _____.
3. He did not _____ the alarm ring.
4. They came to the _____ where the box was.
5. He heard the _____ coming down the street.
6. Pull the hook down _____ and let go.
7. It was the ashman _____ saw the smoke.
8. You must let go of the _____.
9. The _____ knew he must wait at the box.
10. He had saved her _____ for her.
11. Her house had _____ burned down.
12. He hit the _____ to break it.

LESSON 31

LEARN TO READ THE SAFETY SIGNS

The man who works next to Sam had a bad accident the other day in the factory. He had not been to school, and so he had not learned to read the safety signs. He did not close the elevator door.

Over the elevator there is a sign, CLOSE THE DOOR. Mr. Brown could not read that sign, and he left the door open. The next time he went to the elevator, the door was open, but the elevator was not there. It was on the next floor. Mr. Brown walked through the open door and fell down two floors.

They picked him up from the floor and sent him to the hospital. He was hurt badly enough so he will have to be in the hospital for a few weeks.

After the accident, the foreman came to see if each one of the men could read. He said they must learn to read the safety signs in the factory or they could not work there.

The men in the factory put up signs where there is danger. We should know how to read those signs. All the men in the factory who cannot read will have to go to evening school. At school they will learn to read the signs.

They will learn to read the danger signs. Then there will be no accidents, and no one will be hurt.

1. He had not learned to read the _____ signs.
2. CLOSE THE DOOR was over the _____.
3. Mr. Brown left the door _____.
4. The man walked through the _____ door.
5. They picked him up from the _____.
6. They sent him to the _____.
7. He will be in the _____ for a few weeks.
8. The men put up _____ where there is danger.
9. The elevator was on the _____ floor.

LESSON 32

FIRE PREVENTION RULES

1. *Never Let the Children Play with Matches.*
2. *Keep the Matches in a Tin Can Where the Children Cannot Get Them.*
3. *Keep the Ashes in a Tin Barrel.*
4. *Keep Oily Rags in a Tin Barrel.*
5. *Don't Hang Things over the Stove.*
6. *Be Sure Your Match Is Out before You Throw It Away.*
7. *Know Where the Nearest Fire Alarm Box Is.*
8. *Know How to Ring in a Fire Alarm.*

SAFETY RULES

1. *Look Both Ways before You Get off a Car.*
2. *Cross the Street on the Cross Lines.*
3. *Pick Up any Fruit Peels on the Street.*
4. *Don't Keep Rubbish Around.*
5. *Obey the Traffic Signals.*
6. *Don't Let the Children Play on the Street.*

7. *Learn to Read the Safety Signs.*
8. *Never Go Where You See the Sign DANGER.*
9. *Never Let the Children Play or Run with Anything Sharp in Their Hands.*
10. *Look Both Ways before You Cross the Street.*

LESSON 33

REVIEW

1. It was a bad accident because _____.
    the boy had a parcel under his arm
    he did not obey the traffic signals
    the automobiles were going too fast

2. The boy was _____.
    putting stamps on a letter
    reading a book
    putting stamps in a stamp book

3. Mrs. Bruno hung the things _____.
    over the fire   over the stove   out in front

4. The fireman said: _____.
    " Don't hang anything over the stove "
    " All the things are burned "
    " It was not a large fire "

5. The ashman _____.
   - heard the fire alarm
   - went home to his family
   - waited for the firemen to come

6. The ashman _____.
   - rang in the fire alarm
   - ran down the street
   - ran into the house

7. The accident was _____.
   - on the street   in the house   in the factory

8. They sent the man to the _____.
   - hospital   school   factory

9. The foreman told the men they must all _____.
   - ride on the elevator
   - go on new work
   - read the safety signs

10. When you get off a car, you must _____.
    - run across the street
    - look both ways
    - stop and talk with a friend

11. Never let the children _____.
    - go across the street
    - play with matches
    - ride on an elevator

12. The fire engines were ———.
    coming down the street
    going into the house
    stopping at the signals

13. Know how to ———.
    make a fire
    go to the hospital
    ring in the fire alarm

14. Never go where you see the sign ———.
    NO SMOKING
    DANGER
    HELP WANTED

15. The elevator door was ———.
    closed   open   running

LESSON 34

REVIEW

1. It was a bad accident. True   False
2. You must not obey the traffic signals.
   True   False
3. Some stamps cost much money.
   True   False

4. Mrs. Bruno wanted the things to dry.
   True   False

5. The fire engines came down the street slowly.
   True   False

6. The things were not burned.   True   False

7. Always hang things over the stove.
   True   False

8. The ashman takes out ashes.
   True   False

9. The man did not wait at the fire-alarm box.
   True   False

10. An elevator does not move.   True   False

11. Well people are taken to the hospital.
    True   False

12. When the boy was hit, he was hurt.
    True   False

13. No one needs to read the safety signs.
    True   False

14. You do not go where there is the sign DAN–
    GER.   True   False

15. Keep the ashes in a tin barrel.
    True   False

16. Children should play with matches.
    True   False

17. You should cross the street on the cross lines.
    True   False
18. You should pick up fruit peels on the street.
    True   False
19. You should do what the traffic signals tell you.
    True   False
20. You go up in an elevator.   True   False
21. Safety signs are very useful.   True   False
22. A large city has many fire engines.
    True   False
23. There are no hospitals in this country.
    True   False
24. We must never look at the traffic officer.
    True   False
25. The ashman told the firemen where the fire
    was. True   False
26. No one crossed the street when he saw the fire
    engines. True   False
27. A man was badly hurt. True   False
28. Tony did not see a bad accident.
    True   False
29. The man read the sign, CLOSE THE DOOR.
    True   False

LESSON 35

SIGHT READING

THE LAME MAN AND THE BLIND MAN

Once a man who was very lame was walking down a road to the city. He had been walking for such a long time that he was very tired. He was getting more and more lame every mile he walked, and although he was only a few miles from the city, it seemed as though he could go no farther. He saw a large tree by the side of the road, and he went over and sat down under it. He was so tired, he lay down and went right to sleep.

When he woke up, he was surprised to see another man sitting not far from him. He limped over to where the other man was and said: " Good morning, friend. Are you going to the city this morning? I have come a long way and now I am so lame, I can go no farther. Perhaps some one will come along who can carry me."

" Ah, my friend, I, too, have started for the city,

but I am blind. I thought I could find my way alone. I have come this far, and now I am afraid. I shall have to wait for some one to lead me the rest of the way. I had a stick when I started and that helped me to keep on the road. Now I have lost my stick; so I am sitting under this tree waiting for some one to come by who will lead me."

They both sat under the tree feeling very sad, each one wondering how he was going to get to the city.

A happy thought came to the lame man. "I'll tell you what we can do. If you will be legs for me, I will be eyes for you, and we can both get to the city. I can get on your back, and you can carry me. I can tell you which way to go."

This pleased the blind man. The lame man got on the back of the blind man, and they started down the road. The lame man told him which way to go, and before long they both reached the city.

1. Why was the man tired?
2. Why couldn't he go any farther?
3. What did he do?
4. Whom did the lame man see?
5. What did he say to him?

6.   What did the blind man say?
7.   Why did they both feel sad?
8.   What made the lame man happy ?
9.   How did they reach the city?
10. What does the story mean?

LESSON 36

CONTAGIOUS DISEASE

Anna, Tony's child, has been sick for a few days. The doctor says she has scarlet fever. Scarlet fever is a contagious disease; so the doctor has reported it to the Board of Health.

One should always report a contagious disease to the Board of Health. The Board of Health came to Tony's house and put a sign on the door. The sign said CONTAGIOUS DISEASE. Now everyone knows that Anna has a contagious disease and that he must not go to her house.

The doctor says that Anna will have to stay out of school for four weeks. Her brother John will have to stay at home for a few weeks, too. Anna's mother will obey the doctor's orders very care-

fully. She will make John stay out of Anna's room.
John can run the radio for her. He can stay in the
hall and read to her. He can write letters to Anna,
and his mother can give them to her. In this way
he will help Anna and his mother, too.

After the four weeks, when Anna is over the
scarlet fever, the Board of Health will come and
fumigate the house. They will also take down the
CONTAGIOUS DISEASE sign. The Board of
Health always fumigates a house where there has
been a contagious disease.

Then Anna may go back to school. The Board
of Health does all it can to help the people to keep
well. One should always obey the orders of the
Board of Health.

1. The doctor says Anna has ____ ____.
2. It is a ____ ____.
3. The Board of Health ____ ____ ____ ____.
4. The sign said ____ ____.
5. No one may go to ____ ____.
6. Anna must stay out of school ____ ____.
7. John will have to stay ____ ____ ____.
8. Anna's mother will ____ ____ ____ ____.
9. John must not ____ ____ ____ ____.
10. The Board of Health will ____ ____ ____.

LESSON 37

The School Nurse

The school nurse came to see Anna. She wanted to see why Anna was out of school. When she came to Anna's house and saw on the door the sign CONTAGIOUS DISEASE, she knew that Anna was sick. She found out from the doctor that Anna had scarlet fever. She knew that the doctor had reported it to the Board of Health.

John knew the nurse. She had washed his hand one day when he had hurt it in school. They were all glad to see her.

The nurse told Anna's mother that, as John had been exposed to the scarlet fever, he could not be permitted to go to school for a few weeks. This was to protect the other children who were in school. The nurse also said that John must not be permitted to go into Anna's room while she was sick. He would get the scarlet fever, too. Then he would have to stay out of school four weeks.

She told Anna's mother that she must always wash her hands each time she came out of Anna's room. She told her a great many other things that will help her in taking care of Anna. The nurse also told her that, when Anna is better, the house would be fumigated.

The nurse will report to Anna's teacher that she has scarlet fever, for Anna will be out of school for four weeks. The teacher will have Anna's books and papers burned and her desk washed. This care is taken to protect the other children in that room.

The nurse will also report to John's teacher that he has been exposed to scarlet fever and that he will not be permitted to go to school for a few weeks.

The children in her room will send Anna letters through the mail. They may also send her some pictures to look at. Anna will be glad to receive them.

When Anna is well, she will have to have a written permit from the Board of Health before she can go back to school. We should be glad that the city does so much to protect the health of our children.

1. The nurse came to see Anna.   True   False
2. The nurse did not see the sign CONTAGIOUS DISEASE.   True   False
3. She knew the doctor had reported it to the Board of Health.   True   False

4. John would not be permitted to go to school for a few weeks. True   False
5. This was done to protect the other children in school. True   False
6. He could go into Anna's room to read to her. True   False
7. When Anna is better, the house will be fumigated. True   False
8. The teacher will have Anna's books and papers burned. True   False

LESSON 38

THE SCHOOL DOCTOR

Anna is better now. She had to stay out of school for four weeks. John helped her by reading to her each day. The children in her room at school wrote to her, and her teacher sent her a book.

The Board of Health will come today and take down the sign CONTAGIOUS DISEASE. They will fumigate the house. They will fumigate the house by burning a candle in the room. This candle will be burned to kill all the germs. The doors and windows of Anna's room will all be

closed while the candle is burning in her room. All the books and papers which Anna has had while she has been sick must be burned, too. They may have germs on them. This is done to protect Anna's family.

After Anna's room has been fumigated, the Board of Health will give Anna a written permit to go back to school. She will have to report with her permit to the nurse. Every care is taken to protect the children in school.

John had a sore hand the other day; so the teacher sent him to the school nurse. The nurse was not there, but the school doctor was. He looked at the sore hand and told John to put it in hot water every night. Anna's mother will see that he does it, for she wants the hand to get better quickly. The doctor doesn't come to school every day; so the nurse will look at John's hand to see that it is taken care of. If it is best, she will send him to the doctor again.

Our city does all it can to help us take care of the children. We can send them to the school doctor whenever he is at school, and he will tell them what to do. The school doctor doesn't give any prescriptions, but he tells the children if it is best for them to see their doctor.

1. Anna had to stay out of school _____ weeks.

          two   three   four

2. Her teacher sent her a _____.

          dress   book   letter

3. The Board of Health will _____ the house.

          wash   close   fumigate

4. A candle will be burned to kill the _____.

          children   boys   germs

5. This is done to _____ Anna's family.

          expose   protect   permit

6. The Board of Health will give Anna a _____ to go back to school.

          letter   order   permit

7. She will have to _____ to the nurse.
      give   run   report
8. John had a sore _____ the other day.
      toe   finger   hand
9. The teacher sent him to the _____.
      office   nurse   doctor
10. Our city _____ us take care of the children.
      helps   moves   takes
11. The school doctor does not give any _____.
   prescriptions   letters   orders

LESSON 39

HEALTH RULES FOR CHILDREN

The six best doctors anywhere,
And no one can deny it,
Are Sunshine, Water, Rest, Fresh Air,
Exercise, and Diet.

The school nurse told Anna's mother some things to do if she wanted to keep her children in good health. Here are some of the things that she told her:

1. Give them a full bath at least twice a week.
2. Have them clean their finger nails.

3. Be sure they comb their hair.
4. See that their clothes are clean.
5. Make them eat a good breakfast.
6. Have them brush their teeth three times a day.
7. Give them plenty of milk to drink.
8. Give them vegetables and fruit to eat.

LESSON 40

HEALTH RULES

" Health is better than wealth."

1. *Sleep Eight Hours Every Night.*
2. *Sleep with the Windows Open.*
3. *Eat Fresh Fruit.*
4. *Eat Green Vegetables.*
5. *Drink at Least Four Glasses of Water Every Day.*
6. *Wash Your Hands before Eating.*
7. *Take a Full Bath at least Once a Week.*
8. *Brush Your Teeth after Each Meal.*
9. *Keep Your House Clean.*
10. *Keep the Baby Clean.*
11. *Keep the Flies Away from Him.*
12. *Swat the Fly.*

13. *Put the Food Away in the Ice Box.*
14. *Cover Your Mouth with a Handkerchief When You Sneeze.*

LESSON 41

REVIEW

1. The doctor says Anna must stay out of school two weeks.   True   False

2. The sign on Anna's house says PARCEL POST.   True   False

3. Her mother will obey the doctor's orders.
True   False

4. John will have scarlet fever if he goes in Anna's room.   True   False

5. The children in Anna's room at school came to see her.   True   False

6. We should be glad that the city does so much to protect our health.   True   False

7. Anna will take her books to school with her.
True   False

8. The school doctor will give you a prescription when you are sick.   True   False

9. The Board of Health will fumigate the house.
   True   False

10. Anna must have a written permit before she
    can go back to school.   True   False

11. The school doctor tells the children not to see
    their own doctor.   True   False

12. You should swat the fly.   True   False

13. You should take a bath once a month.
    True   False

14. You should have the children in bed every
    night at ten.   True   False

15. You should have the children clean their nails.
    True   False

16. You should sleep with your windows open.
    True   False

17. The mother should keep the baby clean.
    True   False

18. You must obey the doctor's orders.
    True   False

19. You should put food away in the ice box.
    True   False

20. You should sleep eight hours every night.
    True   False

21. You should wash your hands before eating.
    True   False

22. You should eat fresh fruit. True   False
23. You should eat green vegetables.
    True   False
24. You should drink ten glasses of water every
    day. True   False
25. You should never eat vegetables.
    True   False
26. You should not brush your teeth after each
    meal. True   False
27. You should cover your mouth with a handker-
    chief when you sneeze. True   False
28. You should not comb your children's hair.
    True   False
29. You should give your children plenty of milk
    to drink. True   False

LESSON 42

REVIEW

1. What is a contagious disease?
2. What does the Board of Health do?
3. How long will Anna have to stay out of school?
4. What can John do to help Anna?

5. What will the Board of Health do when Anna is well?

6. What can you do to help the Board of Health?

7. Why did the school nurse come to see Anna?

8. What did the school nurse tell Anna's mother?

9. Why does John have to stay out of school?

10. What will the nurse tell Anna's teacher?

11. What will the children in school do to help Anna?

12. What will the Board of Health give to Anna?

13. Why must Anna have a written permit to go back to school?

14. Why does the city do so much to protect the health of the children?

15. How does the Board of Health fumigate a house?

16. Why does it do this?

17. Why do they burn all the books and papers?

18. Why do we have a school doctor?

19. What does he do?

20. What does he not do?

21. How often should your children have a bath?

LESSON 43

Sight Reading

The Ant and the Dove

An ant, walking by the river one day, said to himself: " How nice and cool this water looks. It makes me very thirsty to look at it. I must drink some of it."

He went down to the edge of the water and began to drink. But just at that moment his foot slipped and in he fell. He was very much frightened and cried, " Oh, somebody, please help me or I shall drown."

Up in a tree, whose branches were hanging over the river, sat a dove. She heard the poor little ant and quickly threw him a leaf from the branch on which she was sitting. " Get up on the leaf," she called to the ant, " and you will be able to get ashore."

The ant got up on the leaf and very soon a little breeze came up, and the leaf with the ant on it was blown to shore. The ant stepped off the leaf on to the dry grass.

" Thank you, kind dove, you have saved my life. I should certainly have been drowned. I hope I may be able to do something for you some-time. Good-by, friend," said the ant as he ran off home. " Good-by," called the dove, " be careful not to fall in again."

A few days after this, the ant was again walking by the river, and he saw the dove up in the tree building her nest. A man came by just then and saw the dove. He had a gun with him and was just going to raise it to shoot the dove. The ant saw what he was going to do and ran quickly and bit the man on the leg. The ant bit so hard that the man said " Oh," and dropped his gun. The dove heard the gun drop and flew away. The man picked up his gun and went away, too.

After the man had gone, the dove flew back to her nest. " Thank you, my friend," the dove said to the ant, " you have saved my life. The man was going to shoot me."

The little ant was very happy that he had been able to do something for the dove, for the dove had saved his life.

LESSON 44

Buying an Automobile

Mr. Santo works next to Sam in the factory. He has saved some money in his savings account and now he wants to buy an automobile. He has always wanted to drive one. Mr. Santo has been looking in the paper each night to see if there is an ad of an automobile for sale. He thinks he would like to have a used car and then it would not cost as much as a new one. Last Saturday he went to some of the places where they sell used cars.

Tony knows a man who wants to sell his automobile and maybe Mr. Santo can buy that one. He will go and look at it on Sunday.

Mr. Santo says that, if he buys a car, he will drive it to the factory every day, and that Sam can go with him. Sam will like that, for he will not have to leave home so early in the morning.

Mr. Santo has a wife and three children, and in summer he will take his wife and children out into

the country on Sunday. They can start early and stay all day. Mr. Santo wants to find someone who will sell him a two-door automobile, so he can put the children in the back where they will be safe.

Sam knows that Mr. Santo will like his automobile, for last summer a friend of his bought one, and he used to take Sam and Tony out in it. Sometimes on a summer morning they would start early, take their lunch, and stay all day. They would find a lovely place in the country, and they would have their lunch there.

Last summer one of Sam's friends took a trip in his automobile for his vacation. He went to some very interesting places.

1. Mr. Santo has saved some _____.
2. He wants to buy an _____.
3. He would like to have a _____ _____.
4. He will go and look at it on _____.
5. He will drive it to the _____.
6. Mr. Santo has a _____ and three _____.
7. He wants a _____ _____ automobile.
8. A friend used to take _____ and _____ out.
9. They would go into the _____.

LESSON 45

| STOP | DETOUR |

Tony took Mr. Santo to see the man who wanted to sell his automobile. Mr. Santo looked the car all over, and the man took Tony and Mr. Santo out in it. They went out into the country. Mr. Santo liked the car and decided to buy it. He paid the man $100.00 down and will pay the rest monthly. He is glad he bought a used car.

The man told Mr. Santo that he would teach him to drive. As he works in the factory with

Sam and Mr. Santo, every night after work he takes Mr. Santo out and teaches him to drive the car. Last night when he was teaching him to drive, he took him on a street that had a sign STOP at the end of it. The man told Mr. Santo that he must always stop before he drives out of that street.

There are many streets in the city that have this sign STOP at the end of them. Very often they are short streets that go into a main street where there is much traffic. Anyone driving out of the short street must stop and wait until it is safe for him to turn into the main street. The city puts the sign there, for it wants to protect us.

Another day when the man was teaching Mr. Santo, Mr. Santo was driving. They came to a short street that had the sign STOP at the end of it. Mr. Santo knew that he must stop and look to see if any cars were coming before it was safe for him to drive into the main street.

They went on some other streets, but soon they came to a DETOUR sign. Mr. Santo had often seen this sign and knew that he would often see it again. He also knew that he must follow the DETOUR signs until he would come out on the main road. They followed the DETOUR signs, and soon they were out on the main road.

At the place where there was the DETOUR sign, men were repairing the road. Mr. Santo said that the DETOUR sign was often put up where men were repairing the road. He drove home another way. We must look at the signs, and then we must follow them. They are there for us to read and to obey.

1. Mr. Santo looked the car all _____.
2. Mr. Santo _____ to buy the car.
3. He paid _____ down.
4. He will pay the rest _____.

5. The man is teaching Mr. Santo to _____.
6. STOP was at the _____ of the street.
7. Very often they are short streets that go into a main _____.
8. The city wants to _____ us.
9. Mr. Santo had often seen the _____ sign.
10. He knew he must _____ the DETOUR sign.
11. _____ they were out on the main road.
12. Men were _____ the road.
13. He drove home _____ way.

LESSON 46

NO LEFT–HAND TURN

Yesterday Mr. Santo went to get his license. The man from whom he bought his car has been teaching him to drive. Mr. Santo has been reading the book of rules, too; so he can answer any questions the examiner may ask him.

When Mr. Santo went to get his license, the examiner sat in the automobile with him. He told him to drive down the first street and then to turn left. As soon as Mr. Santo did this, the examiner

told him to stop near the hydrant and to turn.
Mr. Santo went up near the hydrant, but was careful not to go too near it. Then he stopped, and
then he turned.

As Mr. Santo went back down the street, the examiner told him to turn left at the end of the
street. When Mr. Santo came to the end of
the street, he did not turn left as he saw a sign
which said NO LEFT–HAND TURN. The
examiner laughed. He wanted to see if Mr.
Santo could read the signs, and then he wanted
to see if he would follow them. The examiner asked Mr. Santo a few questions about
the rules, and he could answer every one of
them.

The examiner gave Mr. Santo his license. Now he can drive his car anywhere. That night when he went home, he was very happy. In the evening he took his wife and children out for a drive. They were all very happy, too, and the children laughed and looked out of the window.

Tomorrow he will start driving his automobile to work, and he will take Sam with him. They are repairing the road near the factory; so they will have to go on another road. There is a DETOUR sign on the road.

1. Sam went to get his license.   True   False
2. Mr. Santo did not read the book of rules.
   True   False
3. He did not drive too near the hydrant.
   True   False
4. The examiner laughed.   True   False
5. The examiner asked questions about the rules.
   True   False
6. Mr. Santo did not get his license.
   True   False

LESSON 47

NO PARKING

60–MINUTE PARKING

It was about a month ago that Mr. Santo bought his car. He is very thankful that he has his license. He is glad, too, that he could answer all those questions that the examiner asked him about the rules. He has had his license long enough now so that he has no trouble in driving in traffic.

Mr. Santo gets a great deal of pleasure from his car. He takes Sam to work every morning and often takes Sam and Tony out for a drive on their way home. In the evening all the family go out for a while before the children go to bed. A car in summer is very useful and gives a great deal of pleasure.

Last night Mr. Santo took his wife down town to buy some things for supper. Mr. Santo had a good deal of trouble to find a place to park his car. He saw many places where there was the sign NO PARKING, and he knew that he could not park his car there. He went up and down the streets until he found a place near a sign that said 60-MINUTE PARKING. Mr. Santo knew he could buy his things for supper in that time.

He parked his car there while he and his wife went into the store and bought the things for their supper. They were thankful that they had the car and could take the things home in it. It is a good deal of trouble sometimes to take things home on a street car.

On their way home they stopped and took the children out for a short ride. The children sat in the back and were very happy.

1. Mr. Santo bought his car about a week ago.
   True   False
2. He is very thankful that he has his license.
   True   False
3. A car does not give a great deal of pleasure.
   True   False
4. He saw many places where there was a sign
   60-MINUTE PARKING.   True   False
5. It is a good deal of trouble to take things home
   on a street car.   True   False

LESSON 48

SCHOOL—DRIVE CAREFULLY

CURVE   SLOW

Yesterday was Saturday, and the factory was closed for all day. In the morning Mr. Santo and Tony took a ride into the country. They took Mr. Santo's children along with them, but Mrs. Santo couldn't go on the ride, as she had so much work to do.

As they were leaving the city, they went by a

school. It was the school where Mr. Santo's children go. Just before they came to the school, there was a sign, SCHOOL — DRIVE CARE–FULLY. Every one should be careful when he drives by a school. School children may be out in the street. Mr. Santo went on and on for a long while, until they came into the country. It was a lovely ride.

In the country they had no trouble in finding a place to park their car. The children found many flowers by the road, and they picked a great many. One child picked a large handful of white flowers, and the other child picked a large handful of blue flowers. They took the flowers home to their mother. The children knew it would give their mother a great deal of pleasure to have the flowers. They stayed out in the country for a long time.

As they came home, they came to a sharp curve, but there was a sign that told them that they were coming to it. The sign said CURVE. Mr. Santo did not drive fast as they came to that curve. Then they came to another sign. It said SLOW. They went slowly for a way, and soon they saw that men were working on the road.

These signs are put in places where there is danger. They keep people from having accidents. One must not ride so fast that he cannot read the signs.

1. The factory was closed in the morning.
   True   False
2. All the family went to ride.   True   False
3. The children picked some flowers.
   True   False
4. They went fast when they came to the curve.
   True   False
5. Signs keep people from having accidents.
   True   False

LESSON 49

ONE WAY STREET

STREET CLOSED

Mr. Santo lives on a ONE WAY STREET. Automobiles may go up his street, but they may not go down his street. The street is narrow and there would be a great deal of danger if automobiles could go up and down that street. There are many ONE WAY streets down town. The streets are often narrow. Everyone must look at the signs and see which streets he may go up and which streets he may go down.

Last night when Mr. Santo was taking his family out for a ride, one street that they started to go down was closed. At the entrance of the street there was a large sign, STREET CLOSED. It was dangerous for automobiles to go down that street. Men were repairing the street.

Mr. Santo turned down the next street where it was not dangerous and then went on out into a beautiful park. This park belongs to the city, and the city keeps it beautiful for the people. Any one may go there.

In summer this park is just filled with men, women, and children. The children play on the grass, and then they like to go and see the animals. While the children are playing, their fathers and mothers can sit on the grass and rest and read. They like to see the animals, too. All this pleasure costs nothing. The city wants you to come to the park. Anyone may go there and have a good time, and there is nothing for you to pay. The park belongs to you.

When Mr. Santo and his family arrived at the park, the children wanted to play on the grass first.

They played and had a beautiful time. Mr. Santo and his wife rested while the children played.

Mr. Santo saw a traffic officer, and he asked the officer some questions about the park. Later they all went to see the animals. Some of the animals made them laugh.

They all had a very good time, and Mr. Santo says he will take them again soon. He told the children that the next time they go to the park, they may take their lunch and stay all day.

On their way home, the children picked a large handful of flowers to take to their teacher. Just before they arrived home, they came to a sharp curve, but Mr. Santo went very slowly; so there was no danger.

1. Mr. Santo lives on a _____ _____ _____.
2. The street is _____.
3. This park belongs to the _____.
4. The children play on the _____.
5. The mothers and fathers _____.
6. They like to see the _____.
7. Mr. Santo saw a traffic _____.
8. Some of the animals made them _____.
9. They took the flowers to their _____.

LESSON 50

| UNSAFE—AT YOUR OWN RISK |

Mr. Santo knew that he had told the children that he would take them to the park some day and that they could stay all day. Not long after that, there was a beautiful Sunday, and so after church Mrs. Santo put some lunch in a box and they started for the park.

They went a new way this time, so Mrs. Santo could see another part of the city. They had to cross a bridge, but just as they came to it they saw a sign, UNSAFE — AT YOUR OWN RISK.

There had been a heavy rain the night before, and it had made the bridge unsafe. As they did not want to run any risk, they turned and went on another road.

They came to a sharp curve, but it was not a dangerous one and there was a sign CURVE; so Mr. Santo did not drive fast when he came to it. It was a long time before they came to the park.

When they did arrive, they found a place to park their car. Then they got out and took their box of lunch with them. They had so much lunch, that the box was heavy.

The children played and ran on the grass. Mr. and Mrs. Santo sat on the grass and read the paper. When it was time, they went down by some water and had their lunch. The children liked to look at the fish in the water. Some of the fish were very small. They saw some lovely flowers, but they knew that they must not pick any of the flowers in the park.

Before they went home, they went to see the animals again. It looked as if it would rain; so the children picked up all the papers and put them in the box their lunch had been in.

They went home on another road, so that they

would not have to cross on the unsafe bridge. It was late when they arrived home, and it was raining, but they had all had a beautiful time.

LESSON 51

Review

1. Mr. Santo wants to get a _____.

   new car   used car   secondhand car

2. Sam will be glad to go with him, for _____.

   he can start earlier   he likes to ride

   he likes to walk

3. Mr. Santo bought the car because _____.

   it was cheap   it was new   he liked it

4. When you see a DETOUR sign, you must _____.

   follow the sign   go right along   turn

5. The man who sold Mr. Santo his car _____.

   got his license for him   examined him

   taught him to drive

6. The examiner told Mr. Santo to _____.

   drive very fast

   go by the school

   stop near the hydrant

7. When Mr. Santo got his license, he was ＿＿＿.

      unhappy   sorry   happy

8. Mr. Santo is glad that he has his ＿＿＿.

      money   bank book   license

9. At a 60-minute parking place you may park for ＿＿＿.

    half an hour   an hour   30 minutes

10. They took their things home in ＿＿＿.

    the street car   a truck   their auto

11. One must drive carefully by a school because ＿＿＿.

    it is a narrow street

    the children may be out playing

    a traffic officer may be there

12. The children took the flowers to their ＿＿＿.

      sister   father   mother

13. The factory was closed ＿＿＿.

    in the morning   all day   at night

14. Signs are for us to ＿＿＿.

    write about   read   not read

15. From his car one gets ＿＿＿.

    a great deal of money

    a great deal of work

    a great deal of pleasure

16. Men were repairing the _____.

> house   street   dress

17. The park was _____.

> useful   beautiful   small

18. They liked to go to see the _____.

> church   school   animals

19. The fathers and mothers can _____.

> play   rest   walk

LESSON 52

Review

1. In the country there were many flowers.
   True   False.

2. You must drive carefully when you see the sign
   CURVE.   True   False

3. You can go two ways on a one-way street.
   True   False.

4. The city wants to protect us.   True   False

5. Mrs. Santo can go in the country any day.
   True   False.

6. Mr. Santo wants a two-door car.
   True   False.

7. They had their lunch in the water.
   True   False

8. The man did not teach Mr. Santo to drive.
   True   False

9. When you see a STOP sign, you must stop.
   True   False

10. You do not often see a DETOUR sign.
    True   False

11. Mr. Santo stopped next to the hydrant.
    True   False

12. You must turn left when you see the sign, NO LEFT–HAND TURN.   True   False

13. You do not need to read the signs.
    True   False

14. Mr. Santo did not get his license.
    True   False

15. Mr. Santo took his wife with him every morning.   True   False

16. You can park at the NO PARKING sign.
    True   False

17. The schools are open on Saturday.
    True   False

18. The signs are put where there is danger.
    True   False

19. One should look for signs when he is driving.
    True   False
20. SLOW means to go fast.   True   False
21. There are many ONE–WAY streets down
    town.   True   False
22. We pick flowers in winter.   True   False
23. The children do not like to see the animals.
    True   False
24. UNSAFE means not safe.   True   False
25. The children looked at the fish in the grass.
    True   False
26. Some of the fish were very large.
    True   False
27. It looked as if it would rain.   True   False
28. It was early when they arrived home.
    True   False

LESSON 53

A Trip to Washington

It was a beautiful morning when Tony and Sam
started out for their trip to Washington. They
had saved their money by joining a Vacation Club

at their bank. Every Monday night for a long time they had gone down to the bank and deposited some money.

Their bank account grew and grew, until they had enough money to take the trip. All the months they had been saving their money, they had been making their plans. It would take them two days to reach Washington. Tony would drive the first part of the way.

As they left the city and drove out into the country, they were very happy. The birds were singing, the air was warm, and they talked of the many things they were going to see. They were going to see those places of which they had seen so many pictures. They were going to see the places their teacher had told them about. They were going to see the capital of their country.

The roads were fine, and they went right along at forty miles an hour. When they came to a hill, though, they were very careful. They saw the sign, CURVE — SLOW, and they did what the sign told them to do.

When they had gone about ten miles, they came to a sign, STREET CLOSED — DETOUR, but the sign told them which way to go. They followed the sign, and soon they were back on the main road again. They went through some small towns, and they were careful to look out for the signs. They saw the sign, SCHOOL — DRIVE CAREFULLY, and they knew that they must look out for the children.

They made good time and only stopped for a few moments for lunch. In the afternoon they went through a large city. They drove on a ONE-WAY STREET and had a hard time to turn off it. Every street where they wanted to turn left, they saw a sign NO LEFT–HAND TURN. They had to keep on until they came to a street that did not have that sign. They were glad they knew how to read the signs.

Toward night, they came to another large city, and they decided to spend the night there. They found a place where they could put their car for the night, and then they went to a hotel. They had never been in this city before; so everything was new to them.

After supper they went out to walk. There were many bright lights and bright signs, but not so bright as the ones they had seen in New York. They looked in the store windows, and they liked to watch the people. They didn't stay out very late, as they were tired. They went back to the hotel and wrote and mailed some post cards to their friends at home, and then went to bed.

The next morning was beautiful, too. Tony and Sam were up early, for they had many miles to drive that day before they would reach Washington. They wanted to get there before dark.

They were ready to leave the hotel by 7:30, and they started off feeling very gay. Half of the trip was over. They started out on a short street which took them into the main street. Before coming to the main street, they saw the sign STOP. They waited until it was safe to turn into that main street.

Sam drove the second day. He didn't find the roads so good as they were the first day. They had gone only a few miles when they came to a bridge. At the side of the bridge there was a sign, UNSAFE — AT YOUR OWN RISK. Men were repairing the bridge. Tony and Sam went over the bridge very carefully. A traffic officer was there, and he told them when to cross over the bridge.

About noon they came to a small city and stopped for lunch. It was some time before Sam could find a place to park. They saw so many NO PARKING signs. At last they saw a sign that said 6o-MINUTE PARKING. They stopped there, for they knew it would not take them an hour to eat their lunch.

The man in the lunch room told them that they were only a hundred miles from Washington. They were very glad to hear that, for they knew that they could reach Washington in a few hours.

The roads in the afternoon were better, and the country was beautiful. Many flowers were growing along the side of the road.

Before long there was a great deal of traffic, and Tony and Sam knew that they must be near

Washington. They had to drive slowly, there were so many cars on the road.

Soon they saw many large houses. At one place where they had to wait for the traffic signals, they looked down a side street and there in the distance, they could see against the sky, the outline of a tall shaft. Tony saw it first and said: " Look, Sam. See that tall white shaft over there. That must be the Washington Monument. Don't you remember the many pictures we have seen of it? " They were so interested in looking at the monument, they almost forgot to start when the traffic officer signaled them to go.

It did not take them long to get into the city, and they were glad to get there. They had had two long days of driving, and they were tired.

They found a hotel and a place to put the car. They knew what a good time they were going to have in Washington, and they could hardly wait to start out to see the things that they had waited so long to see.

1. What signs did they see on their trip?
2. How long did it take them to go to Washington?
3. How did they know what they were going to see?

4. Where did they spend the first night?
5. What was the first thing they saw in Washington?

LESSON 54

THE CAPITOL

The next morning Tony and Sam were up early. It was their first day in Washington, and they wanted to go first to the Capitol, " the heart of the nation." The clerk at the desk at the hotel told them the way, and as the Capitol wasn't far from their hotel, they decided to walk.

As they walked up Pennsylvania Avenue, they could see in front of them the great dome of the Capitol and the statue of Freedom on top of it. Tony had read that this was one of the most imposing buildings in the world, and as they came nearer to it, they felt that what Tony had read was true.

They saw a beautiful sandstone and marble building which stretched for a whole block in front of them. They saw a large central part of the building under the dome, and on either side of this they saw another part, or wing, of the main building.

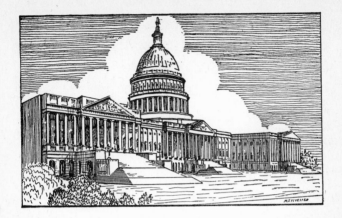

They learned later that it is in these wings, in the Senate and in the House of Representatives, that the laws of our country are made.

They went on and soon found themselves walking through the beautiful Capitol grounds, small parks filled with flowers, walks, trees, and shrubs.

Coming up to this imposing building, they went up the broad steps to the central part of the Capitol, right under the dome at which they had been looking as they walked up the avenue.

As they entered this historic building, they were filled with a great feeling of respect for their country and for the men who had had the courage and strength to be its builders and defenders.

As they were looking at the beautiful paintings

under the dome, a guide came up and asked if they would like to have him show them through the Capitol. Many other people were there, too, and they all followed the guide as he took Tony and Sam around.

The guide first took them to the room where the Supreme Court meets. Tony and Sam knew that this was the highest court of the country and that the nine judges were appointed by the President. As the court was in session, they saw these nine judges, and they were very impressive in their long black robes.

They next went into the Senate. The guide showed Tony and Sam the senators from their state, and they remembered that they had voted for one of them at the last election. They noticed that each senator had a desk and that they were all very busy talking about a new law they were trying to pass.

The guide then took them back through Statuary Hall, where each state has placed statues of two of her great men. Tony and Sam saw statues of some of the famous men that they had read about.

They then went on to the House of Representatives. Here they saw more men than they had seen in the Senate. These men also were very busy making laws.

Tony wanted to stay here in the House of Representatives; so they sat down in the gallery to listen to their own representative, who was talking. When the man had finished, the guide took Tony and Sam to the other entrance to the Capitol.

Here he showed them the place where, every four years, the President of the United States takes his oath of office. The guide told them that thousands of people come from all over the country to see this ceremony. Tony and Sam decided right then that they would plan to take another trip to Washington to see the next president take his oath of office.

LESSON 55

THE WHITE HOUSE

After lunch Tony and Sam went to see the White House. It was a short walk down Pennsylvania Avenue from the Capitol. Sam had read that this was the first public building erected in

Washington. George Washington had laid the corner stone, and although he had seen the building
finished, he had never lived in it.

Long ago it had been burned and only the walls
were left standing. When it was rebuilt, it was
painted white to cover up the marks of the fire.
That is why it is called the White House.

Tony and Sam knew that the President and his
family lived in the White House, and although
they couldn't go into those rooms in which the
President's family were living, there were some re-
ception rooms that people could visit between 10
and 2 o'clock each day.

As it was only 1 o'clock when Tony and Sam
arrived at the White House, they went in to see

these rooms. They saw many beautiful things in these rooms, and among them were valuable gifts that had been received from rulers in foreign countries.

As they came out of the White House, they noticed a low stone building at one side. They asked the guide, who was standing near, what that building was. The guide told them that it was the Executive Offices. Tony and Sam knew that the President was the Chief Executive of the country; so they decided that this was his office.

Tony had read that the President of the United States is the busiest man in the whole country and that one of his duties is to see that the laws of the country are carried out. Tony had also read that the President has ten men to help him. These men are called his cabinet. Each one is at the head of a different department of the government.

Tony and Sam walked back to their hotel through the beautiful White House grounds. Tony's teacher had told him that every Easter Monday the children of Washington, rich or poor, white or black, come to the White House and roll their Easter eggs on the lawns.

LESSON 56

The Washington Monument

As Tony and Sam walked along toward the Washington Monument, they thought of the story of George Washington, the young lad born in Virginia, many years ago when this country was still being settled. They thought of him as a surveyor and of how he went through the deep woods to measure land for the government, meeting fierce Indians and learning how to protect himself against them, and learning also during this time how to be strong and healthy and how to work with other people. They thought also of how, when Washington was older and his country was at war, he led the army and became a great general.

Tony and Sam remembered, too, that when the war was over, he went back to his home at Mt. Vernon. Later the people made him their president — the first President of the United States. They remembered, too, that he was often called the " Father of His Country," that he chose the place for the city of Washington, and that it was named after him.

Coming nearer to this great man's monument, Tony and Sam were unable to speak. It seemed almost sacred to them. The great marble shaft seemed to have the same uprightness and strength that the man had had in whose memory it was built.

They entered the door at the base of the monument and took an elevator to the top. Here they found themselves in a large room with two windows on each of the four sides. From these windows they could see the entire city.

Looking out on one side, they saw a beautiful marble building a short distance away. They knew that it must be the Lincoln Memorial. In front of this building stretched a pool of water with beautiful cherry trees along the sides. It was a lovely sight.

Tony and Sam wanted to go to see it then, but they were too tired. They went back to their hotel very happy that they had seen so many interesting things.

LESSON 57

How Our Money Is Made

" There is one place that I want to go to while we are in Washington," said Sam, " that is the place where the paper money is made."

" Yes, I want to see that too," said Tony, " let's go there this afternoon."

Right after lunch Tony and Sam started out for the Bureau of Engraving and Printing, where the paper money is made. It is a large building down by the Potomac River.

As soon as they went into the building, they found a guide to take them around. First they went into the long room where they saw the paper money being printed. They could see the one-dollar, two-dollar, five-dollar, ten-dollar, and twenty-dollar bills being printed.

" My, I never saw so much money as this, did you, Sam? See, they print four bills on a sheet, and see how fast they count them. I wonder if one person makes a bill."

The guide heard them talking and told them that the paper for the money is made in mills in Massachusetts. " No one knows just how the paper is made," said the guide, " but if you look very closely, you can see some colored silk threads in the new bills. I heard this young man ask if one person made and finished a whole sheet of bills. You see that printer just starting to print that sheet of ten-dollar bills; well, thirty different persons will work on it before that one sheet is finished."

" How much money do they print in a day? " asked Sam.

" Every day they print a million dollars," said the guide. " Every morning at 9 o'clock this million dollars is loaded into a steel truck and under a heavy guard is taken to the Treasury building and put into large vaults until it is sent to the banks all over the country. Perhaps you would like to see the room where stamps are made."

The guide took them into that room, and they saw all the different stamps being printed. Then they saw the machine making the small holes around the stamps, and they saw a machine putting the glue on the backs of the stamps. It was all most interesting to them.

As they came out of the building, they saw the room where the passports are printed.

" I'm interested in that room," said Tony, " because sometime I'm going to Italy to see our relatives, and I shall need a passport. I didn't know they were printed here."

When they came out of the building, they walked along the Potomac River and saw the cherry trees that had been sent over here by Japan.

" Those cherry trees must be beautiful in the

spring," said Sam, "and how friendly it was of Japan to send over all these lovely trees to add to the beauty of Washington."

LESSON 58

SEEING WASHINGTON

The days were going, and there were still many things that Tony and Sam wanted to see. This morning they decided they would take one of the sight-seeing busses and ride all around the city. They knew that there would be a guide on the bus who would tell them about all the things they would see.

They hurried through their breakfast and went out on the street to get a bus. One was just starting; so they got on. It was nearly full, but Tony and Sam found seats with the driver.

" Did you ever see such wonderful streets? " said Sam, as they started on their ride. " It would be fun to drive a car here. The streets are so wide."

First the bus took them by the Capitol. They had been there before, but they were glad to see it again.

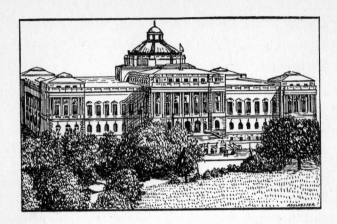

Across the park from the Capitol they saw the Library of Congress. They got out of the bus and went in. Tony and Sam thought they had never seen such a beautiful building. The guide told them that it was one of the most beautiful buildings in the world. Tony was interested in the carved marble stairway, and Sam looked at the brilliant paintings on the walls.

On the second floor they saw, in a case, the original Declaration of Independence and also an original copy of the Constitution of the United States.

"Aren't we glad that we have read about these documents," said Tony. "We would not know what valuable documents these are if we hadn't talked about them in school. See that guard over there?   He watches these valuable documents all day.   The whole government of our country is founded on these papers."

They left the Library of Congress, and the bus took them down Pennsylvania Avenue.   Tony and Sam were very much thrilled when the guide reminded them that they were riding down the same avenue that the President of the United States rides down after he has taken his oath of office.

The bus went by the Treasury building, where, the guide told them, millions of dollars were kept in vaults.   They went by the White House, and just then, the President, in an automobile, came out through one of the gates.   They saw the seal of the United States on the side of his car.

They went by many more public buildings and then out into the part of the city where they saw many beautiful homes.

As they were going by one very large place, Tony said, " Look Sam.   See that flag flying over that fine house.   The flag is red, white, and green.   It's the Italian flag.   I wonder who lives there."

Just then they heard the guide saying: " We are now passing the home of the Italian Ambassador. This house belongs to the Italian government, and the people in it are here to represent the Italian government in the United States."

Tony and Sam felt very proud that their father's government had such a fine place in the capital of the United States. After that they noticed many foreign flags flying over homes, and they knew that the representatives of the countries to which the flags belonged lived in those homes.

As they were riding back through another part of the city, they went by another large white marble building. At one end of the building was the American flag and at the other end of the building was another flag.

When Sam saw it, he said: " Why, Tony, see that flag. It is just like the pin that they give me when I join the Red Cross. That building must have something to do with the Red Cross."

The guide explained to them that it was the Red Cross building, the headquarters of the American Red Cross.

" I'm so glad to see that building," said Tony, " for there is no organization that does so much good as the Red Cross. I always get the men in my factory to join it. I must find my button and wear it."

The bus left the city now and went across the Potomac River.

" This is a fine bridge we are going across," said Sam, " and see how far we can see from it. There is the Monument and the Capitol and the White House, and right over here is the Lincoln Memorial. Just think, Tony, we are really seeing all these things that we have wanted to see for so long."

Across the river they saw miles and miles of grave stones, and the guide told them that this was Arlington, the National Cemetery. Here were buried the soldiers of the Revolutionary War, the Civil War, and the World War.

" What a lot of people to have been killed! " said Sam.

Tony and Sam got out of the bus and walked around to the fine old mansion where General Lee had lived and from which he had gone at the time of the Civil War. General Lee never returned to this beautiful home.

Every one wanted to see the grave of the Unknown Soldier. As they stood in front of it, they all took off their hats in tribute to that brave soldier who had fought for their country.

Tony and Sam wondered if that unknown soldier might have been an Italian. A Polish man who was standing near wondered if that brave soldier might have come from his country. Whoever he was, the greatest possible honor had been given to him.

The bus brought Tony and Sam back to the city, and they were very thoughtful. They had had a fine morning, and they had seen so many of the places which they had heard so much about.

"Tony," said Sam, "I never realized before what a wonderful country this is. I never thought before, either, about the great number of men that have died so that the rest of us might live in a peaceful country. We have seen that Declaration of Independence, and we have seen all those graves at Arlington and the grave of the Unknown Soldier. You and I must do all we can to help to keep this country peaceful, and as fine as it is beautiful."

"Yes, we must," said Tony. "The success of any country depends upon the courage, industry, and character of the citizens of that country."

"America stands for 'liberty and justice for all.' Its citizens have courage, industry, and character. We must do our part to make this country successful."

LESSON 59

Abraham Lincoln

That night Tony and Sam went to the movies. When they came back to the hotel, they sat down to read about Abraham Lincoln. They were going to visit the Lincoln Memorial the next day.

They read that Abraham Lincoln was a very poor boy, born over a hundred and twenty years ago in a log cabin in the back woods of Kentucky. He had few books, and he had no chance to go to school. His mother taught him to read. She taught him to write and to make figures. He had no pencil or paper, no pen or ink. He wrote with

a piece of charcoal on the back of a fire shovel. He
would sit on the floor in front of the fire and read
by the light of a pine knot. As a boy he learned
to do very difficult things and to do them well. He
learned how to be honest and how to play fair.

They read, too, that Lincoln grew to be a great
man. He loved all the people, and he believed in
them. He believed that everyone should be useful
and happy. His state needed him to help with its
problems, and finally the whole country needed
him and he became the President of the United
States.

They read that while he was president he had
many very difficult things to decide — things so difficult that if they were decided one way, it would
mean war, but if they were decided another way, it
would mean a weak and divided country and a weak
and divided people. All through Lincoln's life he
had had courage, always knowing that there are
two sides to every question; so when these difficult
questions had to be decided, he always tried to see
both sides.

They read that it is to Abraham Lincoln that
we owe the greatness of our country, for it was he
who kept us a United States of America.

The next morning when Tony and Sam went to
see the Memorial to this great man, they saw a
very magnificent building, one that did credit to
this fair-minded, honest, and kind man.

Around the four sides of the building were thirty-
six columns representing the thirty-six states which
were in the Union at the time that Lincoln was
president.   Above these were carved forty-eight
wreaths, representing the forty-eight states which
are in the Union now.

They walked up the broad flight of steps into the
central hall where there is a huge marble figure of
Abraham Lincoln seated in a chair.   As Tony and
Sam stood before this huge figure, they took off
their hats and stood in silence, thinking of what
this one man had meant to their country.

On the walls of a small room next to the one con-
taining the figure of Lincoln is carved one of the
most famous speeches ever made in this country.
Tony and Sam read every word of this speech of
Abraham Lincoln's.

" Tony," said Sam, " we are going back home
tomorrow, but we shall never forget this trip to
Washington.   We shall go away remembering all
these things that we have seen and remembering

also the debt that we owe to Lincoln and to all those other heroes who lived and died that this country should be a ' government of the people, by the people, for the people.' "

As they walked back to the hotel, they made their plans for their trip home, and they decided that they would go back by way of Gettysburg, so that they might see the national cemetery where Abraham Lincoln had made his famous speech.

LESSON 60

Topics for Discussion

1. The Legislative Branch of the government.
2. The Executive Branch of the government.
3. The Judicial Branch of the government.
4. Contrast the inauguration of a foreign ruler with that of the President.
5. The Oath of Office of the President.
6. Diplomatic etiquette in this country.
7. Washington's home in Mt. Vernon.
8. Contrast the social life of the first President and that of the President of today.
9. The Declaration of Independence.

10. The Constitution of the United States.
11. Natural resources of our country (gold and silver).
12. Where our gold money is made and kept.
13. Where our silver money is made and kept.
14. How long a new one-dollar bill will last.
15. Why the cherry trees were sent to Washington.
16. Why there are foreign representatives in this country.
17. What the Red Cross does.
18. The grave of the Unknown Soldier.
19. Why Lincoln is one of our heroes.
20. Heroes of foreign countries.
21. The Gettysburg speech.
22. What makes a man a hero.
23. How you would go by auto from your city to Washington.
24. What you would most want to see in Washington.

LESSON 61

REVIEW

1. Tony and Sam saved their money in the bank.
   True　　False
2. They had been to Washington before.
   True　　False
3. They had heard about the places in Washington.　True　　False
4. It took them three days to get to Washington.
   True　　False
5. They wrote post cards to their friends.
   True　　False
6. They did not stay at a hotel.　True　　False
7. They went around the city on a bus.
   True　　False
8. The Library of Congress is a small building.
   True　　False
9. They saw the Declaration of Independence.
   True　　False
10. It is not a valuable document.　True　　False

11. The money is kept in the Capitol.
    True   False
12. They saw where the Italian Ambassador lives.
    True   False
13. The Italian flag is red, white, and blue.
    True   False
14. The Red Cross does much good.
    True   False
15. They saw the grave of the Unknown Soldier.
    True   False
16. Tony and Sam thought they lived in a wonder-
    ful country.   True   False
17. They wanted to see where the paper money is
    made.   True   False
18. The stamps are printed in the Treasury.
    True   False

LESSON 62

REVIEW

1. The Capitol is sometimes called " the heart of
    the nation."   True   False
2. The Washington Monument has a dome on top
    of it.   True   False

3. The President has his office in the Capitol.
    True   False
4. All the people in the Capitol are busy making laws. True   False
5. The Supreme Court is the highest court in the land. True   False
6. The judges are elected by the people.
    True   False
7. The White House has been burned once.
    True   False
8. George Washington laid the corner stone of the White House. True   False
9. People may go into all the rooms in the White House. True   False
10. The children roll their eggs at Christmas.
    True   False
11. The Executive Offices are for the judges.
    True   False
12. George Washington was the first President of the United States. True   False
13. He was a soldier in the Revolution.
    True   False
14. Abraham Lincoln never went to school.
    True   False

15. He always looked on both sides of a question.
    True   False
16. He made a famous speech.   True   False
17. The President lives in the White House.
    True   False
18. Lincoln said that we should have a " govern-
    ment of the people, by the people, for the
    people." True   False

A

a
about
ad
ads
admittance
again
all
A.M.
am
and
any
are
arrive
arrived
arriving
at
avenue

B

be
been
Boston
bought
boy
boys
bright
brother
but
buy

C

came
caps
car
careful
cars
Chicago

children
church
city
come
coming

D

day
days
dear
decided
depot
did
didn't
do
door
doors
down
dress
dresses

E

East
employment
English
entrance
evening
evenings
every
exit

F

factory
family
father
find
fire
first
for

foreman
found
Friday
friend
friends
from

G

girl
girls
glad
go
going

H

had
has
hat
hats
have
he
help
helped
helping
her
him
home
house
houses

I

I
Illinois
information
in
into
is
it

J

John

K

know

L

last
learn
learned
leaving
left
letter
like
liked
likes
look
looked
love
lovely

M

Main
man
many
Massachusetts
may
me
men
Michigan
Monday
month
morning
mother
move
moved
movies
must
my

N

New York
new
next
night
no
not

O

of
office
on
one
other
out

P

paid
paper
pay
people
picture
pictures
P.M.
pull
pulled
push
pushed
put

R

radio
radios
read
read
reading
rent
room
rooms

S

said
sale
sales
Saturday
saw
school
see
seen
September
shall
she
sign
signs
sister
smoke
smoking
so
some
something
State
stop
stopped
store
stores
street
streets
suit
suits
Sunday

T

take
telegram
telegraph
that
the
theater

theaters
their
them
there
they
thing
things
those
three
Thursday
ticket
tickets
to
today
told
tomorrow
too
took
town
train
trains
trip
truly
Tuesday

U

until

W

walk
walked
walking
want
wanted
wants
was
way
we
Wednesday

week
well
went
were
what
when
where
which
will
window
windows
with
woman
women
work
worked
would
write

Y

yes
yesterday
you
your
yours

A

accident
account
across
alarm
also
amount
animals
answer
as
ashman
ask
automobiles

B

back
bad
bag
bank
beautiful
before
best
better
bills
blank
blue
Board of Health
book
box
break
bridge
brown
building
burned

C

can
candle
card

cash
check
Christmas
city
cities
clerk
closed
club
contagious
corner
cost
could
country
curve

D

danger
dangerous
department
deposit
disease
deal
detour
doctor
does
doesn't
dollars
drive
dry

E

each
early
elevator
end
engines
enough
examiner
exposed

F

fast
fell
fever
few
fill
floor
flowers
follow
four
front
fumigate

G

gave
germs
get
glass
good
got
grass
great

H

hand
handle
hang
happy
hear
heard
heavy
his
hit
hook
hospital
hung
hurt
hydrant

I

if
interested
Italy

J

joined
just

K

kill
knew

L

large
late
laugh
letter
license
listening
long
lost
lunch

M

made
mail
make
meet
minutes
money
much

N

narrow
near
noise

nothing
now
nurse

Q

question

O

obey
officer
often
once
open
order
our
over
own

P

parcel
park
paying
permit
picked
places
play
pleasure
possible
post
prescriptions
protect

R

rain
receipt
receiving
registered
repairing
reported
rest
ride
ring
risk
road
rules
run

S

safe
safety
sat
save
says
scarlet
sell
send

sharp
shoes
short
should
sick
signaled
since
sit
slip
slowly
small
son
soon
sore
spend
stamps
started
stay
stove
summer
supper

T

teach
teacher
teller
ten

thankful
thought
through
top
traffic
trouble
turn

U

unsafe
up
us
used

V

vacation
very

W

wait
wash
water
while
white
who
why
wife
wrote